Thank you.
Enjoy!
bb

Our Father Who Aren't in Heaven

Yours in the cause of justice,

Robert Hunter

Our Father Who Aren't in Heaven

Subversive Reflections on the Lord's Prayer

ROBERT S. TURNER

Foreword by Gregory Bezilla

WIPF & STOCK · Eugene, Oregon

OUR FATHER WHO AREN'T IN HEAVEN
Subversive Reflections on the Lord's Prayer

Wipf & Stock
An Imprint of Wipf and Stock Publishers
199 W. 8th Ave., Suite 3
Eugene, OR 97401

www.wipfandstock.com

ISBN 13: 978-1-4982-0097-4

Manufactured in the U.S.A.   02/11/2015

For Sarah Cee

Contents

Foreword

"THE LORD'S PRAYER, WHILE arguably the most universally accepted and practiced element of Christian worship, is also one of the most misunderstood," writes Bob Turner. "How many of us understand the subversive, even revolutionary character of what we are praying?"

Be very careful—you've been warned. This book will change your understanding of that most routine of prayers. The one we say at weddings and funerals. The one we know by heart. The one we say at the close of contentious committee meetings, when we're verbally exhausted and spiritually spent. The one we fumble when we've had too much to drink. Our comfort prayer.

Yet there's comfort aplenty in Bob Turner's interpretation of the Lord's Prayer. Good news for the poor in spirit and the poor. It has power to set the captives free. This is a book that will give you eyes to see more clearly what God is doing in the world and to hear God's call to the church.

Bob Turner is a Baptist preacher who interprets the Lord's Prayer through the lens of Scripture. He isn't making this stuff up! It's in the Bible, and it's right there in the prayer that Jesus taught his disciples.

Be ye comforted. This is not an angry book, or a new-fangled, theory-driven attempt to debunk our orthodoxies. You'll read in these pages a faithful witness to the God of justice, mercy, and compassion. You'll meet the God who gave us Jesus—a prophet who spoke the Word and was the Word, the Holy One acknowledged by devils and confessed by sinners and outcasts as Savior and Lord. It's a trustworthy witness to the Resurrection, and to the Spirit that still fuels faithful discipleship and does impossible things like overthrow apartheid.

It turns out that theology is a help to spirituality. When we say the Lord's Prayer we benefit from knowing what is in and under those familiar words we mutter in the pews or with our heads on our pillows. Knowledge really is power. Best of all, the insights and understandings offered by this accessible book speak volumes to those big issues that fill the headlines and disturb our rest. Thanks be to God.

The Reverend Gregory Bezilla
Chaplain, Rutgers Canterbury House
New Brunswick, New Jersey

Acknowledgments

EVERY WRITER WITH EVEN a dash of humility knows that, although much of the writing process takes place in solitude, writing is ultimately not a solo effort. Around each writer stands, in the words of the Epistle to the Hebrews, "a great cloud of witnesses" (Heb 12:1), some living, some dead, who can claim credit for at least part of what gets put down on paper. Each of us learns, borrows, and absorbs much from thinkers who have gone before, and from the influences of teachers, friends, loved ones, and so on. All these contributions get stirred up and mixed together until it is next to impossible to tease out the various influences and say precisely where one's ideas have come from.

Of course, if I were to list and thank everyone who has influenced me over the years and formed me into who I am today, these acknowledgments would run longer than the actual book. So I will limit my comments to those who have played the most direct role in inspiring and supporting this writing project.

I thank my copyeditor, Catherine Kaser, for her excellent work on my manuscript. I also want to thank Matthew Wimer, Laura Poncy, Ian Creeger, and all the good folks at Wipf and Stock Publishers who have helped bring my book to light. Their flexibility, patience, and willingness to go out on a limb for an unknown author evoke—and deserve—my deep gratitude.

My friend Greg Bezilla offered me encouragement and feedback, and served as a sounding board and enthusiastic conversation partner. His insights helped me hone my ideas and my writing, and he has been one of this book's cheerleaders from early on.

Three communities of faith deserve special mention. First, Ravensworth Baptist Church in Annandale, Virginia, will always hold a special place in my heart. It was the site of the slip of the tongue that provided the title of this book, but far more importantly, the ethos of this vibrant church, its energy, and its attitude of welcome and inclusion continue to give me a glimpse of what church can be. My time there offered healing of old hurts and sparked a renewal of my commitment to the kingdom of God. Ravensworth's unofficial motto, "Sharing love, doing justice, and building community," perfectly captures the spirit of this wonderful group of people.

Second, I want to thank the members of Christ Congregation in Princeton, New Jersey, who welcomed me into their midst during a time of transition and uncertainty. I am especially grateful to pastor Jeff Mays and to Charles McCullough, who not only connected me with Wipf and Stock, but also gave me the opportunity to flesh out some of the ideas in this book during "Second Hour."

Third, I am grateful to First Baptist Church of Cooperstown, New York, who helped me get back into active parish ministry by calling me to be their interim pastor. They have welcomed me to this beautiful area of their state and to their congregation with warmth and enthusiasm. And what could be better than living within walking distance of that great shrine, the National Baseball Hall of Fame and Museum?

I thank everyone who contributed to this project through their prayers, encouragement, wise counsel, and, in some cases, financial support. These include Eleanor Brosius, Adam and Carey Ensminger, Brian Hall, Kristin Dare Horsley, Marshall Marks, Pamela Grenfell Smith, Liz Ward, and Judy Popper Williamson. My sincerest thanks to you all.

A good deal of the writing and revising of this book coincided with a frustrating period of unemployment for me. My family sustained me during this time and gave me the motivation I needed to keep going. My father- and mother-in-law, George and Ruth Councell, have done more for Sarah and me than we could ever repay, and they did it out of love. My mom, Doris Turner, has been cheering me on for longer than I can remember, even when I was sure I didn't deserve it. My daughters, Natalie and Rachel, never stopped believing in me, and I am so proud of the young women of faith, integrity, and passion they have become. I love you all deeply.

Finally, I have to acknowledge my wife, Sarah. She has enriched my life to an extraordinary degree in the last ten years, and I dedicate this book to her. I wrote the book, but in so many ways, every day of her life, Sarah *lives* it. She inspires me to be the best husband, disciple, and man I can be, and she contributed in very practical ways by reading my manuscript and giving me her feedback. Sarah doesn't pull any punches, and I found some of her comments difficult to hear. But besides all her other wonderful qualities, Sarah is one of the wisest people I know, and in almost every case in which she thought I had gone too far, or not far enough, I took her advice. This book is much stronger because of her perspective. Thank you, Sarah. I love you.

Robert S. Turner
Cooperstown, New York
September 2014

Permissions

Introduction

Listening As We Pray

THE LORD'S PRAYER. THE Pater Noster. The Our Father. The Disciples' Prayer. It goes by many names, but it is perhaps the one thing Christians the world over have in common. Nearly all Christians observe Communion, or the Eucharist, or the Lord's Supper, but in widely variant ways and with very different understandings of its significance. Likewise, baptism takes a number of different forms and opens itself to different interpretations. The Bible—well, don't even get me started on the Bible. Catholics, mainline Protestants, Evangelicals, and the Orthodox can't even agree on which books belong in the Bible, and the interpretation of the books they do agree on produces some of the most virulent intra-religious conflict in the church today. Many Christians recite the same creed, but others, including those of the Baptist tradition to which I belong, don't accept the authority of the creeds. I only ever say the words of the Nicene Creed when I worship in an Episcopal church with my wife's family, and when I do I always feel furtive about it. Even a little guilty. Hymnody, liturgy, style of preaching, and the language we use for God all vary from denomination to denomination and from church to church, and are as likely to divide as to unite Christians.

But every Sunday the world over, Christians of every color, language, and hermeneutical leaning say the words of the Lord's Prayer. True, there are some differences—some say "trespasses" while others say "debts," some say "forever and ever" at the end of the prayer while others close with the more concise "forever," and Roman Catholics omit the concluding doxology. But these variations do not throw up any major obstacles to Christian comity and unity the way the different expressions of the Eucharist do, for example. The Lord's Prayer seems to unite rather than divide Christians all around the world. With the possible exception of the ancient confession, "Jesus is Lord," nothing else in the Christian tradition can make such a sweeping claim.

Anything that can make a claim of binding together more than two billion Christians from mud huts to mansions, war zones to strip malls, First World to Two-thirds World and all points in between, will also, by its very nature, claim remarkable familiarity. Our circumstances, locations, and languages may differ, but at the heart of our shared faith lies a shared prayer that in its most familiar English version runs like this:

> Our Father who art in heaven,
> hallowed be thy name.
> Thy kingdom come, thy will be done
> on earth as it is in heaven.
> Give us this day our daily bread
> and forgive us our debts (trespasses)
> as we forgive our debtors (those who trespass against us).
> And lead us not into temptation
> but deliver us from evil.

Most Protestants add this doxology:

> For thine is the kingdom and the power and the glory forever (and ever). Amen.

Of course, anything that becomes overly familiar runs the risk of losing its power. When we repeat the Lord's Prayer for the umpteen thousandth time, we may fail to reflect deeply on the meaning of every phrase and clause. It's like saying the Pledge of Allegiance; at some point in childhood we stopped wondering what "indivisible" meant and just said it and got on with our lives. I suspect we very often do the same with the Lord's Prayer: " . . . for thine is the kingdom and the power and the glory forever, amen"—and now let's move on.

As an example of how easy we find it to stop hearing what we're saying, try this experiment: read the prayer above aloud, choosing your preferred version when it comes to debts and trespasses and the extra "and ever" at the end. Did you notice anything odd about the prayer? Anything incongruous?

Now, you may have been on the alert because I called it an experiment, and if so, you may have noticed that the most common form of the Lord's Prayer in English uses antiquated language—words and sentence structures that we use very rarely if at all in modern English. Words such as "thy" and "thine," and clauses such as "hallowed be thy name" and "thy kingdom come" would have a strikingly unfamiliar ring if we heard them in any other context. But because they appear in this most familiar Prayer, we roll them off our tongues without a second thought. Familiarity breeds . . . not contempt in this case, but at least a form of deafness.

In the chapters that follow, I will try to crack the hard shell of that familiarity and hear these old, old words in a new way. Or rather, in a way that may seem new, but that actually represents an effort to get back to the context in which Jesus first taught his disciples the Prayer and in which they first heard it. In the subtitle of this book, I call these subversive reflections on the Lord's Prayer. That's because this most familiar, most seemingly tame of prayers could very well be the most radical and revolutionary manifesto to come to us from Jesus's time or any time. To take these words seriously might change our lives in profound and permanent ways, and to act on them might have the capacity to shake the foundations of the world.

Does that sound like an overstatement? Have I set myself too ambitious a goal? Maybe. On the other hand, maybe we underestimate the power of the Lord's Prayer because so many of us have long since stopped expecting anything of it. We have long since stopped listening as we pray. To unlock the tremendous potential waiting inside these words, we must act on them. To act on them, we must first hear them. And to really hear them, we have to listen.

I invite you to listen along with me.

The Empty Hammock

Our Father who art in heaven . . .

I CAN'T PUT MY finger on precisely when it first happened, but not that long ago, I heard myself utter a malapropism right there in worship one Sunday morning. As the senior pastor finished up the prayers of the people, he gave us the cue we had all been listening for: " . . . as Jesus taught us to pray . . . " and we launched into the Lord's Prayer. With the rest of the congregation, I said, "Our Father who aren't in heaven. . . ."

Wait a minute. What did I just say? It's supposed to go, "Our Father who *art* in heaven." Art. Not aren't.

I found this slip of the tongue troubling, but in my defense, the wording of the original is pretty odd. If we updated it to modern English, we would say, "Our Father who are in heaven," which would be grammatically incorrect. We would more properly say, "Our Father who is in heaven," or, more concisely, "Our Father in heaven." Instead, we can thank the translators who produced the King James Bible for bequeathing to us an antiquated and syntactically wrong phrase that has since lodged itself durably in the Christian lexicon.

Plus, it sounds a lot like "Our Father who aren't in heaven"—an impious statement at best, if not a fully blasphemous one.

Or is it? As I thought about it (and now I can't help but think about it every time I pray the Prayer), it struck me that there may be more truth to that verbal blunder than first appears. Far from denoting some kind of atheistic anti-creed, like the title of Christopher Hitchens's book, *God Is Not Great*, it may actually say something profoundly apt about God.

CHANGING GOD'S ADDRESS

When I think of "Our Father who aren't in heaven," I recall one of the first scenes in *Romero*, the 1989 film about Oscar Romero, Archbishop of San Salvador, starring Raul Julia. The movie traces the progression of Romero from a bookish and fairly conservative Roman Catholic bishop to a firebrand preacher and activist. Converted to liberation theology, which proclaims that God has a "preferential option for the poor," he seeks to empower the oppressed Salvadoran peasants in their struggle for justice. Romero's embrace of this politically charged brand of theology leads directly to his assassination. Death squads in the employ of the government or the army or the oligarchy (precisely who ordered his murder has never been definitively established) shot and killed him as he celebrated the mass in March 1980.

In this early scene, Romero has gone with his friend, Father Rutilio Grande, to observe a voter registration drive led by some young people from Father Grande's parish. While there, he overhears what to him sounds like radical, even sacrilegious talk, and he expresses to Father Grande his concern for him and his teaching. He says that some in the church have accused Grande of holding extreme views. Romero finds the idea so alarming that he stammers as he says it: "Some are saying that you are a sub-subversive."

Grande replies, "Remember who else they called such names." To make sure we don't miss the point, he goes on to say, "Jesus is not in heaven somewhere lying in a hammock. He is down here, among his people, building a kingdom."[1]

Of course, Father Grande is exaggerating to make a point. If you pressed him, he would undoubtedly acknowledge the classic Christian affirmation that Jesus, following his resurrection and ascension, ascended to heaven and now sits "at the right hand of the Father." Jesus *is* in heaven. God is in heaven. Yet with equal conviction we can say that in a powerful

1. "Subversive," *Romero*, 1989.

and important sense they *aren't* in heaven. At least not lying in a hammock, as though they have finished their work and have nothing left to accomplish down here.

Saying "Our Father who aren't in heaven," then, does not deny the divinity or exaltation of God or Jesus. Rather, it affirms that they are not *only* there. When we imagine the heavenly location of God too rigidly, we run the risk of failing to see God at work on earth. But a short step from there lies Deism—the notion of God as a sort of absentee landlord, a Creator who set the world in motion according to scientifically discernible natural laws and then took a long lunch break and still hasn't returned.

Planting God too firmly on some heavenly throne emphasizes the transcendence of God at the expense of God's immanence. Christianity has always held these two attributes of God in balance. God indeed transcends all creation. We cannot comprehend God's majesty. "[God] dwells in inapproachable light" (1 Tim 6:16). "The Lord, the Most High, is awesome, a great king over all the earth" (Ps 47:2). "How great thou art." "A mighty fortress is our God." The contemporary church, at least in North America, suffers from an overfamiliarity with God. It behooves us to maintain a vision of God as one "sitting on a throne, high and lofty . . . the hem of [whose] robe [fills] the temple" (Isa 6:1).

But the Christian faith has always held God's transcendence in tension with a conviction of God's nearness and accessibility. Throughout salvation history, God has always acted as the initiator. God approaches Abraham with the promise that he will be the ancestor of a great nation. God speaks to Moses face-to-face, as one speaks to a friend. God enters into an extravagant, passionate covenant with David. Finally, God comes into the world as a human being for the purpose of effecting our salvation once and for all. Add to all this the activity of the Holy Spirit, who moves within individuals and communities to continue the work Jesus began, and you have a picture of a God as close to us as our own skin.

To be accurate, then, we should say both, "Our Father who aren't in heaven," *and*, "Our Father who art in heaven." God is both high and lifted up and intimately present with us.

Psalm 139 captures this dual reality in extraordinarily beautiful language. The psalmist extols the majesty and immensity of God's being:

> How weighty to me are your thoughts, O God!
> How vast is the sum of them!
> I try to count them—

they are more than the sand (vv. 17–18 TNIV).

This God whose thoughts cannot be counted fills the whole universe, so that trying to get away from God's presence is futile:

> Where can I go from your Spirit?
>   Or where can I flee from your presence?
> If I ascend to heaven, you are there;
>   if I make my bed in Sheol, you are there.
> If I take the wings of the morning
>   and settle at the farthest limits of the sea,
> even there your hand shall lead me,
>   and your right hand will hold me fast (vv. 7–10).

Those last two lines are telling. In spite of the absolute immensity and ubiquity of God, the psalmist does not hesitate to extol God's closeness: "Your right hand will hold me fast." This language of intimacy continues:

> You search out my path and my lying down,
>   and are acquainted with all my ways.
> Even before a word is on my tongue, O LORD,
>   you know it completely.
> You hem me in, behind and before,
>   and lay your hand on me (vv. 3–5).

This intimate knowledge of God's goes back even before the psalmist's birth:

> My frame was not hidden from you, when I was being made in
> secret,
>   intricately woven in the depths of the earth.
>   Your eyes beheld my unformed substance.
> In your book were written all the days that were formed for me,
>   when none of them as yet existed (vv. 15–16).

This magnificent psalm, with its deft interweaving of God's transcendence and immanence, prefigures the Christian doctrine of the Incarnation. The prologue of the gospel of John, with its very high Christology, locates Jesus, whom John calls the Logos, or "Word," with God before creation. John goes so far as to *identify* Christ with God: "In the beginning was the Word, and the Word was with God, and the Word was God. He was in the beginning with God. All things came into being through him, and without him not one thing came into being" (John 1:1–3a). That's a pretty exalted view of Christ—as the very agent of creation and, indeed, as a full partner in the Godhead. As the Nicene Creed puts it, "The only Son of God . . . Light from Light, true God from true God."[2]

Yet the story John has to tell in his gospel will not allow Christ, the Logos, to remain in this transcendent state. Instead, "The Word became flesh and made his dwelling among us" (John 1:14 TNIV). With this affirmation John leads us to the brink of one of the most powerful mysteries of our faith: how could Jesus be a mortal man but also God? Or, to put it another way, how could God enter into the human experience and still be God?

Jesus's followers shared the conviction that something about their teacher set him apart from everyone else. They saw that the Spirit and Wisdom of God filled him in a unique way and they felt privileged to witness it—"We have seen his glory" (John 1:14). From these convictions developed the idea that later became the doctrine of the Incarnation. As the church of the first few centuries grappled with the question of how Jesus could be one with the Father—how the Word could not only be *with* God, but could also *be* God—the companion doctrine of the Trinity developed. These two mysteries, the most distinctive theological affirmations of the Christian faith, bring together the transcendence and immanence of God in a powerful way. God is high and lifted up, so we can say with conviction that God art in heaven. Because of the life, death, and resurrection of Jesus—the Word become flesh—and the subsequent gift of the Holy Spirit, we can affirm simultaneously that God *aren't* in heaven.

With the Incarnation, God in a sense filled out a change-of-address form. No longer could we conceive of God as distant, inscrutable, and inaccessible. No longer could we understand God as *only* transcendent, or as removed from the lives and concerns of God's creatures. When God was born into the world as a human baby to human parents, whether in a house or in a cattle shed or under any other imaginable circumstances, God's address changed. Or, more accurately, God established a dual residence.

Our Father who art in heaven.

Our Father who aren't in heaven.

---

2. For the text of the Nicene Creed and a line-by-line explication of its meaning, see World Council of Churches, *Confessing the One Faith*, 10–12, 44.

THE HEAVEN GHETTO[3]

As modern (or postmodern) people trying to read and interpret the Bible, we face the difficult challenge of removing many accumulated layers of tradition and misinterpretation to get to what the authors really meant. We have a tendency to forget that the Bible hails from the ancient world. Because many Americans still live in a religion-saturated culture, and because the Bible remains a perennial bestseller, we may perhaps be excused for thinking of it as a contemporary word for our contemporary times. After all, that's what countless Sunday School classes and Bible study groups—at least in the evangelical world—encourage us to do: to learn how to "apply the truths of the Bible to our lives."

This can be dangerous, however, if we fail to make the appropriate translations. By this I don't mean simply verbal translations from the ancient Greek of the Christian Scriptures and the ancient Hebrew and Aramaic of the Hebrew Scriptures into contemporary English or Hindi or Mandarin. This is important, of course, and many reputable translators continue to produce accessible and reliable versions of the Bible for modern readers. But we must not translate only the words. In fact, we court danger when we translate the words and fail to translate the meanings and the cultural and historical contexts of the words. We must do this second kind of translation if we want to understand what the biblical writers sought to convey and how their first readers understood their writings.

Over the centuries, contexts have changed. The meanings of words have changed. The sociological setting of many of the Bible's readers has changed. Layers upon layers of cultural and literary sediment have built up until we cannot be certain of the "plain meaning of the text" any longer. The responsible student of the Bible in many ways resembles an archaeologist sifting through the strata of an excavation, seeking to get past the encrustations of later years and find the original site. Sometimes one uses a shovel and a pick, sometimes a whisk broom, and sometimes a fine-haired brush to clear away the intervening layers. We may want to identify the sources of those layers—to flag and label strata from different centuries or

---

3. By my use of the word "ghetto," I mean to imply only a place where a group is segregated by choice or by force, not a place of poverty or crime. My friend Greg Bezilla, Episcopal chaplain at Rutgers University, suggests that the common understanding of heaven more resembles a community where the privileged are protected. He calls it a "pearly-gated community." Bezilla, Personal correspondence, 2014.

eras—but we must always keep in mind our ultimate goal: to get to the original stratum.

For a good example of the danger inherent in failing to do this sort of "archaeological" work, consider the concept of heaven. Over the centuries of Western civilization, we have developed some persistent and culturally enforced notions about the existence and nature of heaven. Some of these notions are serious, some are silly, and some are plain wrong, but many of them hold powerful sway over our collective imagination to this day. The images of winged beings with halos lounging on clouds and playing harps we may easily spot as pop-culture notions with no basis in the Scriptures of either Israel or the church. Unfortunately, they have become deeply embedded in the popular imagination. If you doubt the iconic nature of such images, consider how often they appear in comic strips, cartoons, and advertisements—three pretty reliable gauges of our cultural imaging.

Other ideas about heaven may not be quite so harmless. Many people conceive of heaven as some sort of spirit world where our disembodied souls dwell before our birth and return after death (if we have been "good" or have met God's requirements during our lives). This idea may seem to resonate with Paul's description of "spiritual bodies" in First Corinthians 15, but it actually contradicts the Hebraic notion of the unity of spirit, soul, and body, and fails to take seriously the ancient understanding of resurrection. Paul shared both of these convictions. The Apostle's Creed, the most ancient of all confessions of the Christian faith, proclaims the resurrection of the body. The idea that my body merely serves as the earthly house or container for the real me, my soul, and that once my body dies my soul will be freed to return to God, holds more in common with Greek philosophies such as neo-Platonism than it does with the faith of Jesus or Paul.

But perhaps the most dangerous thing about our "de-contextualizing" of heaven is the way we have turned it into a sort of holy ghetto. When we over-spiritualize heaven, locating it in some distant, otherworldly Never-Never Land, and confining it to serve as the final destination of "good" or "saved" people after their deaths, it becomes irrelevant and safe. It begins to resemble a make-believe place that no intelligent or sensible person really believes in. Even worse, the powerful have cynically exploited this understanding of eternal postmortem reward, of "pie in the sky by and by," for centuries. Consider the slaveholders who fed their slaves this otherworldly notion of heaven as an incentive to remain meek and obedient. Think of the preachers in the pocket of moneyed interests, who served thick slices of this pie to their working-class congregants in an effort to focus their gaze on heavenly bliss and take it off of their living and working conditions. Remember the white clergymen of Birmingham who, from their comfortable and insulated nests, chastised Martin Luther King Jr. for pushing too hard for justice. Not without reason did Karl Marx identify heaven-based religion as the "opium of the people." An otherworldly, postmortem reward for the humble and manipulable can indeed have a numbing, narcotic effect.

But did the biblical writers really have this in mind when they talked about heaven? More to the point, since one of the two places in the New Testament that a version of the Lord's Prayer appears is the gospel of Matthew (the other is Luke), what did Matthew mean when he used the word "heaven"?

Matthew, or the writer of the gospel bearing that name (we don't know for sure who actually wrote it), was from all indications a pious Jewish Christian. His church—the congregation for whom he wrote his gospel—apparently comprised Jewish and Gentile Christians, so Matthew took great pains to present Jesus as the Savior of both Jews and non-Jews. But Matthew himself was almost certainly a Christian of Jewish heritage.

Several pieces of evidence from his gospel back up this claim. For one, in Matthew 5 Jesus says, "Do not think that I have come to abolish the Law and the Prophets; I have not come to abolish them but to fulfill them. Truly I tell you, until heaven and earth disappear, not the smallest letter, not the least stroke of a pen, will by any means disappear from the Law until everything is accomplished" (Matt 5:17–18). Throughout his gospel Matthew emphasizes Jesus's respect for the Law.

Matthew also makes frequent use of prediction-and-fulfillment formulas throughout his gospel. We see this especially clearly in the birth narrative of the first two chapters, but examples run all the way through the story of Jesus's passion. Matthew often says, "All this happened to fulfill the word of the Lord spoken by the prophet," before quoting a passage from the Old Testament and then demonstrating its fulfillment in an episode from Jesus's life.[4] This concern to prove that Jesus fulfilled the Scriptures of his people bespeaks a Christian writer who takes pride in his heritage as a Jew.

But the example that touches our present topic most directly is Matthew's reluctance to use the word "God." Many modern writers, mindful of the commandment against taking the Lord's name in vain, write "G-d" instead of "God," and those reading the Bible in Hebrew say "Adonai" when

---

4. See, for example, Matthew 1:22, 2:15, 8:17, 12:17, 13:35, and 21:4.

they come across the name YHWH, instead of pronouncing the word "Yahweh." In the same way, Matthew clearly feels uncomfortable writing the word "God" in his gospel. He draws heavily on the earlier gospel of Mark in composing his own gospel, but he seems to find Mark's frequent use of the word "God" careless or irresponsible. As a result, Matthew replaces Mark's signature phrase, "the kingdom of God," with a circumlocution, "the kingdom of heaven."

And that is where we run into trouble.

When Mark used the phrase "kingdom of God," he had in mind a very this-worldly phenomenon. He was talking about a state of affairs in which God's creatures acknowledge God's sovereignty over the world. God rules with justice and equity, and puts all other powers, such as human monarchs or nation-states, in their proper relation to God and the people they represent, or else removes them. In the kingdom of God, oppression, injustice, greed, and other abuses of power give way to freedom, security, sharing, and equality. Mark depicts Jesus as the proclaimer and first realization of the coming kingdom of God. In his ministry the first shoots of the kingdom begin forcing their way through the soil of the world, and Mark imagines a time when those few shoots in an arid and dusty land will become lush vegetation that covers the whole world. As the Christmas song "O Holy Night" says in reference to Jesus, "In his name all oppression shall cease."[5]

I have been using the phrase "kingdom of God" because it is the most common translation of the Greek phrase *basileia tou theou*. Many Christian thinkers, however, have begun moving away from that wording and saying instead the "reign of God." They cite at least two very good reasons for doing this. First, it removes the troublesome patriarchal term "kingdom" from the mix. Feminist theologians rightly object to the uncritical use of terms such as "Father" or "King" to describe God, because they inappropriately attribute maleness to God. This reinforces men's traditional domination of women and fails to acknowledge feminine aspects of the divine.

Second, "reign of God" better communicates the dynamism Jesus intended. "Reign" signifies a state of affairs rather than a static place. Jesus, and Mark after him, imagined God gaining more and more sovereignty over the world as more and more people accepted God's reign. In Mark's gospel, Jesus describes the spread of God's reign using the metaphor of a pinch of yeast that over time works its way through an enormous batch of dough until all of it is leavened. "Reign" speaks of movement and action.

5. Dwight, "O Holy Night."

"Kingdom," by contrast, makes it easy for us to imagine a *place* where God is king, much as the United Kingdom is the place where Elizabeth II is queen and Saudi Arabia is the place where Abdullah is king. "Kingdom" smacks of stasis. When we understand God's "kingdom" in this way, we think we know its precise geographic location. In the ghetto we call "heaven," once we have God safely tucked away in "his" kingdom, we can quite happily ignore it and get on with running our own kingdoms any way we see fit.[6]

Matthew shared Mark's convictions about the role and reality of the growing, dynamic, insistent reign of God. Unfortunately for us, he quite piously substituted the circumlocution "heaven" for "God," and unwittingly helped to reinforce the static and safe notion of the heaven ghetto—precisely the opposite of what he believed or intended.

Too long have we perpetuated the idea of a postmortem reward in the next world for those who play nice and don't rock the boat down here. It is imperative that we reclaim Mark's and Matthew's (and Jesus's) dynamic vision of the reign of God as the growing sovereignty of God's justice, peace, security, and abundance in this world. The heaven ghetto holds no relevance for persons who suffer under oppressive regimes in North Korea and Zimbabwe, who live in war zones in Afghanistan and the Democratic Republic of Congo, or who face persecution for their religious beliefs and practices or for simply asserting their basic human rights in Iran and China. The idea of a heavenly ghetto mocks those who every day bury another child shot and killed in Chicago, who watch their hopes for their children's futures dry up in a small town in the Rust Belt, or who struggle with addiction, depression, and ennui in a Manhattan penthouse. The vague promise of heaven carries little weight for those who already live in hell. What they want and need is a living hope that God sees them where they are, cares about what they are going through, and is actively moving to bring into being a just and peaceful reign that will transform their lives here and now.

Those of us who have heard and responded to the call to join God's team enjoy the privilege of participating in the realization of God's reign. Not later, in some unearthly paradise after death, but now, in the muck and mire and heartbreaking beauty of this world God made and still loves passionately and fiercely.

6. In this book I will frequently use the phrase "kingdom of God" because of its traditional usage and greater familiarity, but always with the more dynamic sense of "reign" described above. In a similar way, my use of the term "Father" for God relates to the wording of the Prayer and should not be construed as an endorsement of patriarchalism but only a concession to familiar usage.

Our Father who aren't in heaven. It's time to liberate God from the ghetto.

A SAFE GOD, POCKET-SIZED FOR YOUR CONVENIENCE

A God confined to a heavenly ghetto is a safe God. Safe as in predictable. Safe as in manageable. Safe as in tame.

Nothing at all like the God described in the Bible variously as a consuming fire (Ps 97:3), as one who is resplendent with light (Ps 76:4) but surrounded by clouds and thick darkness (Ps 97:2), and as one whose mysteries are unfathomable. Such a God is mysterious, holy, wild, and free. And not at all to our liking. We don't want a God whom no one has seen or can see (1 Tim 6:16). We want a reliable, comfortable, familiar God. A God we can carry around in our pocket.

Karen Peris of the Innocence Mission captures this penchant of ours with poignancy and grace in her song "Every Hour Here." She sings:

> You are like the ticket-half
> I find inside the pocket of my old leaf-raking coat.
> There all the time, all the while, forgotten.
> . . .
> I take the ticket-half
> and put it on the table, saying
> This is God
> and he is here through my comings
> and my goings.
> But I walk past the ticket-half,
> I walk past the ticket-half
> just as I've walked past the cross
> on our wall.[7]

We want the kind of God we can slip into our pockets or leave, as Peris says, "in churches and other islands." We want a safe, predictable God, pocket-sized for our convenience. By confining God to the heaven ghetto, by placing the ticket-half on the table where we can keep tabs on it, we foster the illusion that we have some control over God. Like the Deists with their missing divinity, we incarcerate God in an irrelevant heaven and claim for ourselves the right and responsibility to run things as we see fit on earth. In another scene from *Romero*, the Archbishop and the

7. The Innocence Mission, "Every Hour Here," 1991.

Jesuit Provincial meet with the President-elect of El Salvador. When the President-elect complains that the priests have been meddling too much in politics, the Provincial says, "But there are political implications to the gospel." The President-elect narrows his eyes and says, "We will take care of those."[8]

That is why it is so important for us to liberate God from the heaven ghetto and liberate ourselves and others from the theology of a pocket-sized God. There have always been, are now, and will continue to be those who are more than willing to step into the gap left by such a God and run the show to their own liking. An honest self-assessment might show that we are that way ourselves. The political implications of the gospel represent a clear threat to those of us who benefit from the status quo. In order to preserve that status quo, we will "take care of" the political implications, by which we mean we will ignore them, or discredit them, or manipulate and warp them so they work in our favor. The ideological milieu that can produce millionaire preachers of a "prosperity gospel" who boast that their "garages runneth over"[9] has a vested interest in keeping God safe, tame, and either on our side or so inconsequential that it doesn't matter *whose* side God is on. "I walk past the ticket-half / just as I've walked past the cross / on our wall."

But Scripture and our collective experience describe a wild, untamable God who remains always free and capable of doing something new. As Jesus told Nicodemus in reference to the Spirit of God, "The wind blows where it chooses" (John 3:8). God is still speaking, and God is always liable to say something new and unexpected: something that has the power to shake our foundations and push us into the uncomfortable position of having to re-evaluate and re-imagine our most basic understandings and assumptions about God.

No wonder we find it so tempting to keep God at a manageable size or tucked away in the irrelevancy and predictability of the heavenly ghetto. Especially when the present system works just fine for us, thank you very much. Who wants a pesky God coming around and messing up all our neat theological categories, or worse, our political agendas or financial portfolios? Let us just put the ticket-half in our pocket where it can be safely ignored.

---

8. "Violence," *Romero*, 1989.

9. Blake, "Was Jesus Rich?," para. 17.

Ironically, it is often precisely in defense of God (we claim) that we reject many of the new things God tries to say. Take for instance the hot-button issue of whether gays and lesbians can be full members of society in general and the Christian community in particular. Should we accept and affirm them just as they are, or does God demand that we stigmatize and marginalize them until they repent of the "sin" of being gay? Those who opt for conditional acceptance and the necessity of repentance often back up their arguments by appealing to certain scattered passages of Scripture such as Leviticus 18:22, Romans 1:27, and 1 Corinthians 6:9–10. Those who wish to accept lesbian, gay, bisexual, and transgender (LGBT) persons as full members of the community without reservation believe the broader witness of the Bible proclaims God's unconditional love for all of God's children. Even if some parts of the Bible appear to support a more restrictive view, they maintain that God always remains free to speak a new word now.

In this and many similar debates, it boils down to a question of how we understand the Bible. Do the Scriptures present the literal, and therefore inviolate, words of God? Are they free of cultural relativity to such an extent that they remain eternally valid for all people, everywhere, at all times, without exception? Or do the Scriptures bear witness to the convictions of various people and communities in antiquity and to their culturally and historically conditioned *understanding* of God? Do they reflect what those people thought it meant to live in covenant relationship with God? If so, would it not follow that we, too, have the capacity to interpret our understanding of and relationship with God in the contemporary world in ways just as valid for our time as their interpretations were for their time, *even if we come to different conclusions* than they did?

This is not a new problem. We find evidence of this tension in the pages of the Bible itself. Take the Babylonian captivity, for instance—one of the three most traumatic experiences in the history of the oft-traumatized Hebrew/Jewish people. (The other two were the destruction of Jerusalem in the first century and the *Shoah*, or Holocaust, in the twentieth.)[10] When the Babylonians forced the people of Israel into exile in the sixth century BCE, it necessitated a fundamental reevaluation of the covenant between God and Israel.

10. Some Jewish leaders have expressed objections to the use of the word "holocaust" to describe the Nazis' program of extermination because, in the Torah, the term refers to the practice of sacrificing burnt offerings to God. As an alternative, they have suggested *Shoah*, a Hebrew word meaning "catastrophe" or "calamity."

For the Israelite people, the land (*ha-aretz*) was central to their self-understanding and their relationship with God. According to Genesis, God promises the land of Canaan to the patriarchs Abraham, Isaac, and Jacob, and a good chunk of that book and the next several books of the Old Testament relates how God overcomes a series of seemingly insurmountable obstacles to keep that promise. Obstacles such as infertility, famine, slavery, war, and the people's unfaithfulness threaten again and again to derail the project, but God remains faithful and keeps the divine end of the bargain.

After the rise of the monarchy in the eleventh century BCE, a new wrinkle appears. God makes an extravagant and practically unconditional promise that King David will have a perpetual dynasty. God tells David through the prophet Nathan, "Your house and your kingdom will endure forever before me; your throne will be established forever" (2 Sam 7:16).

Now, in one fell swoop, the Babylonian army's conquest of Jerusalem, destruction of the Temple, and removal of the majority of the people from the land have put a sudden end to both of these covenants. The people are separated from the land of promise and the last king of David's line, Jehoiachin, dies in exile.

We perhaps cannot fully appreciate the earth-shattering, catastrophic nature of these events. For those of us who are Americans, it would take something like the violent overthrow of our government by a hostile foreign power, the repudiation of the US Constitution, and the outlawing of Christianity to approximate the shock and dismay the people of Israel experienced in the wake of the Exile.

After the Exile, the religious leaders, theologians, and prophets face the daunting task of finding a way to put the pieces back together. They find, however, that the Israel they knew before has shattered, Humpty Dumpty-like, and they cannot fix it. The old categories simply don't fit anymore. There is no going back.

When we read the prophetic books composed in the years during and after the Exile, we find a radical reformulation of Israel's relationship with God. The theological and poetic genius behind chapters 40–55 of the book of Isaiah, who wrote in the post-exilic period and has been dubbed by scholars "Second Isaiah," provides a perfect example of this re-thinking. Speaking for God, this prophet says:

> Forget the former things;
> do not dwell on the past.
> See, I am doing a new thing!

Now it springs up; do you not perceive it? (Isa 43:18–19).

Tellingly, this counsel not to dwell on the past comes after Second Isaiah has just recounted Israel's exodus from bondage in Egypt and their deliverance from the pursuing Egyptian army at the Red Sea, pivotal events in the story of how God keeps the promise to give Abraham's descendants the land of Canaan. This part of the biblical record has embedded itself in the national DNA of the Israelite people, yet Second Isaiah tells them to forget it. "Do not dwell on the past." God is getting ready to do something new, something unheard of, something outside all the categories and definitions that characterized the past—even the sacred past.

God is still speaking, the prophet says, and God has the freedom to say and do something utterly new. Something that drastically reworks or even contradicts what has gone before. Nothing and no one can handcuff God—not even Scripture. God is free.

The New Testament also shows evidence of this tension. Peter's experience in the household of Cornelius in chapter 10 of Acts represents a sea-change no less thorough or drastic than that accompanying the Babylonian Exile.

The story begins with Peter staying at the home of a tanner named Simon in the city of Joppa. Luke, the writer of the book of Acts, is trying to tip us off from the very outset that something unusual and unexpected awaits. Because tanners regularly and necessarily come into contact with dead animals, many pious and observant Jews consider them perpetually unclean from a ritual standpoint. For Peter to lodge in a tanner's house provides a clue to what is to come.

It's almost lunchtime, and Peter is starting to get hungry. On the roof of Simon's house, he prays and meditates while he waits for the midday meal to be prepared. During his prayers, Luke says, Peter falls into a trance and sees a vision of a sheet being lowered down to him from heaven. The sheet holds every kind of unclean animal—pigs, snakes, owls, jumbo shrimp—all the animals the Torah forbids the Hebrew people to eat, as recorded in Leviticus 11. It's a veritable smorgasbord of impurity.

After the sheet comes down, Peter hears a voice from heaven telling him, "Get up, Peter. Kill and eat" (Acts 10:13). Peter responds almost immediately, as though offended by the very thought: "Surely not, Lord! I have never eaten anything impure or unclean" (Acts 10:14).

In response, the voice says, "Do not call anything impure that God has made clean" (Acts 10:15), and the sheet gets snatched back to heaven.

The same vision comes twice more, and Peter presumably gives the same answer each time. Luke does not describe the manner of his responses, but one suspects Peter's staunch refusal to eat the taboo food may show signs of wavering the second and third times. The brash self-confidence of his first answer has slipped a bit by vision number three. Peter spent plenty of time with the enigmatic Jesus and can remember several times when he was sure he knew the right answer to a question, only to have Jesus pull the rug from under his feet, demonstrating in no uncertain terms that Peter's answer was emphatically, embarrassingly wrong.

But he feels he stands on pretty solid ground this time. The first five books of the Hebrew Scriptures, the Torah, form the basis of the Jewish people's common life and survival. The Torah is one of the elements—the *central* element—that holds the community together. It tells the stories of the nation's origins, the enslavement of the people and their deliverance in the Exodus, and the giving of the Law. If anything in the traditions of the Hebrew people is holy and inviolate, it's the Torah.

But now Peter hears a heavenly voice—presumably that of God or Jesus—telling him to break the kosher laws that spell out in great detail which foods are acceptable and which are off-limits. Could it be that God has changed the rules? Or, more likely, Peter concludes, this is just a test from God—or a temptation from the devil—to see if he will remain faithful to the rules he has always known. After all, didn't Jesus himself face the temptation to turn stones into bread when he was hungry? Perhaps the real lesson is not to meditate on an empty stomach.

While Peter puzzles over these questions, messengers from Cornelius, a Gentile centurion stationed down the Mediterranean coast in Caesarea, arrive at the house of Simon the tanner. They have come looking for Peter, per God's instructions, so he can bring Cornelius the good news about Jesus. According to Luke, God tells Peter to welcome the men and then to accompany them back to Caesarea. Peter has the good sense to do as he is told.

When they reach Caesarea and enter Cornelius's house, they find the centurion and his cultured Gentile guests expectantly awaiting the great apostle's arrival. Peter demonstrates his gift for flattery and tact when he immediately announces, "You are well aware that it is against our law for a Jew to associate with Gentiles or visit them" (Acts 10:28a). One imagines the assembly glancing at one another after this introduction, trying to decide whether to be offended or amused. But Peter salvages the situation, at least partially, by continuing, "But God has shown me that I should not call anyone impure or unclean" (Acts 10:28b).

The penny has dropped for Peter. Somewhere along the way from Joppa to Caesarea, he finally gets it. The vision of the sheet was not about animals and keeping kosher at all. It was about people and relationships. It was a new word from God that the distinctions that had mattered so much in the past—clean and unclean, Jew and Gentile—must keep God's children apart no longer. Even when the distinctions are set down in Holy Writ, God remains free to do a new thing.

God does that new thing, and puts a divine seal upon this declaration of God's freedom, in a dramatic way. Peter begins telling those gathered at Cornelius's villa the story of Jesus, and how he offers forgiveness of sins. He hasn't even finished his sermon, however, when something strange happens. Peter's audience of *uncircumcised Gentiles* suddenly begins speaking in other languages and praising God. These same phenomena accompanied the coming of the Holy Spirit to the Jewish believers at the feast of Pentecost (see Acts 2). Peter and his Jewish Christian companions from Joppa connect the dots and come to the conclusion that the Spirit has indeed come upon these Gentiles. Peter takes this realization the logical next step and says, "Surely no one can stand in the way of their being baptized with water. They have received the Holy Spirit just as we have" (Acts 10:47). Peter baptizes Cornelius and the group of new believers without further delay.

Sometimes it takes something as dramatic as this for us to acknowledge God's freedom to say and do something new. Sometimes it takes a long, slow, plodding advance—an advance not without its times of retreat and retrenchment—and the patient guidance of the Spirit to get us to see what God has been trying to show us. Sometimes great evils get committed because of our resistance to God's freedom, and sometimes awful tragedies are the price of that resistance. Sometimes the prophets' lonely voices cry in the wilderness for years before the world finally hears and heeds their message.

One thinks of William Wilberforce, who led a prolonged crusade against the slave trade in Parliament for more than two decades before enough others shared his conviction to abolish that evil practice throughout the British Empire. One thinks of Frederick Douglass, Harriet Tubman, Ralph Waldo Emerson, Lucretia Mott, and others who pounded the drum of abolition in America, and for all those who toiled for years before them who did not live to see the fruits of their labors. One thinks of Desmond

Tutu, Nelson Mandela, Lilian Masediba Ngoyi, and Steve Biko in South Africa; Lech Walesa and the leaders of Solidarity in Poland; Alexander Solzhenitsyn, Irina Ratushinskaya, and Andrei Sakharov in the Soviet Union; and Martin Luther King Jr., Fannie Lou Hamer, John Lewis, Rosa Parks, Medgar Evers, and countless others who waged the long struggle for civil rights in America. Some of these saw victory, others died while still in the struggle, but all held tenaciously to the idea that God was free to say and do something new. Despite all the appeals to Scripture in favor of the status quo by their opponents, these and others stood firm in the conviction that God does not will that some human beings should enslave other human beings. They kept up the struggle because of their conviction that God does not will that one group of people should be systematically shut out of decision-making, wealth, and opportunity because of the color of their skin. They fought long and hard because of their belief that God wants all people to be free.

Some have won their battle. For others, the struggle continues. Salvadorans still seek the just peace for which Oscar Romero and Rutilio Grande died. Aung San Suu Kyi, now a Member of Parliament, continues her campaign for freedom and democracy in Burma. Dissidents in China, such as Chen Guangcheng and Liu Xiaobo, continue their dogged campaign to win political freedom for their people. Organizations such as Amnesty International and Bread for the World keep mobilizing citizens in the United States and Europe to secure human rights for all and to end poverty and hunger around the world. And ordinary citizens carry on the often uphill struggle to live their lives from day to day with peace, security, dignity, and freedom.

All these people, whether they know or acknowledge it or not, live, work, and struggle under the constant gaze of a God who longs to pour the Spirit on all flesh. This God is neither aloof and distant nor tame and manageable. This God is not sequestered in a heavenly ghetto, or in churches and other islands. This God moves among us, walks beside us, gently pushes us forward, and beckons us to follow as God leads us into a new and unknown future where the only certainties are that God is free and God is love.

PREFERENTIAL OPTIONS

If God has indeed broken out of the heaven ghetto and acts in and among us here on earth, what is God doing? And if God is always free to do a new thing and speak a new word, can we possibly know or predict what that might be? One of the fears that prompts us to try to lock God away or maintain God at a manageable size is the fear of unpredictability. When the children hear about Aslan, the great Lion of Narnia, for the first time, in C.S. Lewis's *The Lion, the Witch, and the Wardrobe*, Susan nervously asks their guide, Mr. Beaver, "Is he—quite safe? I shall feel rather nervous about meeting a lion."

"Who said anything about safe?" Mr. Beaver snaps. "'Course he isn't safe." He is, after all, a lion. "But he's good. He's the King, I tell you."[11]

Like many people, I fear the unknown, and the unsettled feeling I get when I realize I am not in control sends me running after security at almost any cost. One of the places I look for that security is in religion. If God intends to upset that applecart and push me into even *greater* uncertainty, I will not be pleased. It's wonderful that God is good, but what I really want is a God who is *safe*. Perhaps my experience resonates with your own.

If so, it is important for us to continually remind ourselves of God's consistency and dependability. While God *is* always capable of doing and saying something utterly new, we find that even these new things are consistent with God's character as we know it through the Scriptures and from our own experiences. Jesus revealed God as *Abba*, a loving, nurturing, and intimate parent who knows the number of the hairs on our heads and cares for us beyond measure.

Influenced as he was by the classical Hebrew prophets and by his mentor John the Baptist, Jesus also revealed God's passion for establishing justice for all God's children. Although we have tended, at least since the Enlightenment, to focus on Jesus's message to us as individuals, most responsible interpreters now understand Jesus and his message in broader social terms. Instead of seeing Jesus's work as saving individual sinners from hellfire, we would do better to speak of him as the founder of a movement whose aim was to establish a new kind of community where justice and equity reigned. Evangelical Christians like to ask their non-Christian neighbors the question, "If you died tonight, do you have the assurance that you would be in heaven tomorrow?" A better question, and one more faithful to Jesus the radical social prophet, might be, "If you *don't* die tonight, what will you do tomorrow to help create a more just, peaceful, and livable world?"

We see this in the gospel of Mark, where Jesus proclaims his signature message: "The time is fulfilled, and the kingdom of God has come near;

11. Lewis, *Lion, Witch, and Wardrobe*, 80.

repent and believe in the good news" (Mark 1:15). Mark reports this as a summary of the content of Jesus's preaching early in the first chapter of his gospel, and then spends the next fifteen-plus chapters demonstrating what he thinks Jesus meant by it. He shows Jesus casting out demons; performing healings; feeding large crowds in the wilderness; teaching and preaching; welcoming sinners; and treating women, lepers, Gentiles, the upper crust, and the dregs of society as equals. He also spends a fair amount of time in confrontations with religious leaders—sometimes responding to their accusations and sometimes bringing indictments of his own. In fact, just such an offensive—a head-on collision with the priestly aristocracy and the representatives of Roman imperial power—occasions his violent death at the hands of those powers.

Matthew and Luke both draw heavily on Mark in composing their gospels, and they continue and expand Mark's depiction of Jesus as a prophet of justice. Matthew reports that Jesus says in his Sermon on the Mount, "Strive first for the kingdom of God and his righteousness [or justice], and all these things [the necessities of life] will be given to you as well" (Matt 6:33), and, "Blessed are those who hunger and thirst for righteousness [or justice], for they will be filled" (Matt 5:6).[12] Luke, for his part, has Jesus begin his public ministry with a proclamation of social justice. He reports that in Jesus's inaugural sermon, in which he sets forth his agenda and mission for his entire ministry, he quotes (loosely) a passage from Isaiah 61. Luke's version goes like this:

> The Spirit of the Lord is upon me,
> because he has anointed me
> to bring good news to the poor.
> He has sent me to proclaim release to the captives
> and recovery of sight to the blind,
> to let the oppressed go free,
> to proclaim the year of the Lord's favor (Luke 4:18–19).

Taken together, Mark, Matthew, and Luke paint a composite portrait of Jesus as one who cares deeply about this-worldly issues such as hunger, disease, oppression, poverty, and injustice, and who presumes that God

---

12. The Greek words for "justice" and "righteousness" are very close in meaning, as are the corresponding words in Hebrew. The righteousness Jesus talks about in these verses is not the righteousness of personal piety or rule-keeping, but rather social righteousness—doing right in all of one's dealings with others. Because in English "righteousness" most often refers to *personal* righteousness, I find it helpful to use the word "justice" instead, since that word communicates the social element more clearly.

shares these concerns. This is no other-worldly Savior sent forth from the heavenly ghetto with the mission of snatching people out of the world so they (or their souls, anyway) can spend eternity within the bounds of that same ghetto. This is a prophet—sometimes a firebrand prophet—sent by God to prepare *this* world for the coming of God's reign. The locus of Jesus's and God's work is not heaven. It's here.

For an illustration of this, consider one of the clauses from that inaugural sermon in the fourth chapter of Luke. Jesus declares that part of his mission is "to bring good news to the poor" (Luke 4:18). It may actually be too weak to call this *part* of Jesus's mission. From its position at the head of the list of activities the Spirit has empowered him to perform, Jesus may mean for this clause to control, or set the bounds for, the clauses that follow. In other words, it may be that the subsequent activities—"proclaiming release to the captives, and recovery of sight to the blind," and so on—simply elucidate what "good news to the poor" looks like. By this reading, Jesus considers his *primary* purpose to tell the poor God's good news of liberation.

This understanding of Jesus's mission gave liberation theology—an important, influential, and controversial way of talking about the Christian faith—its name. Arising in the 1970s and 80s, primarily in Latin America, liberation theology made a bold and, to some, a shocking declaration: that God has a "preferential option for the poor."

This phrase signifies that God profoundly cares about the lives of those living in poverty and other oppressive circumstances, and that God makes their relief and freedom God's first order of business. "The Spirit of the Lord is upon me to bring good news to the poor." Not surprisingly, many people who have been conditioned, consciously or unconsciously, by the notion that God either has the same regard for everyone equally or, less innocuously, that God actually prefers the rich, have taken umbrage with the whole liberation theology project. Isn't wealth, after all, a sign of God's favor? Doesn't God want us to prosper? For those who hold these views, liberation theology is to be feared and, whenever possible, discredited.

In response, liberation theologians say these objections indicate that those who express them have benefited from the systems that hold their poor neighbors in bondage, and therefore have a vested interest in protecting those systems from overhaul or correction. For liberation theology, as for Jesus, there is no middle ground: "Whoever is not with me is against me," he said (Matt 12:30).

The roots of liberation theology go back farther than the ministry of Jesus. The Old Testament, the Bible Jesus knew, veritably teems with examples of God's particular care for the disadvantaged and marginalized. In Exodus 22:22–23, for instance, God gives this instruction concerning the most vulnerable members of ancient Israelite society: "Do not take advantage of a widow or an orphan. If you do and they cry out to me, I will certainly hear their cry." Deuteronomy 10:18 (TNIV) says of God, "He defends the cause of the fatherless and the widow, and loves the foreigners residing among you, giving them food and clothing." Deuteronomy 24:17–18 instructs the people to imitate God's stance toward the poor: "You shall not deprive a resident alien or an orphan of justice; you shall not take a widow's garment in pledge. Remember that you were a slave in Egypt and the LORD your God redeemed you from there; therefore I command you to do this."

Other passages from the Hebrew Scriptures emphasize the same or similar themes, as we see in these passages:

> When you reap the harvest of your land, you shall not reap to the very edges of your field, or gather the gleanings of your harvest. You shall not strip your vineyard bare, or gather the fallen grapes of your vineyard; you shall leave them for the poor and the alien: I am the LORD your God. (Lev 19:9–10).

> O LORD, you will hear the desire of the meek;
>   you will strengthen their heart,
>   you will incline your ear
> to do justice for the orphan and the oppressed,
>   so that those from earth may strike terror no more (Ps 10:17–18).

> Look, you serve your own interest on your fast day,
>   and oppress all your workers.
> Look, you fast only to quarrel and to fight
>   and to strike with a wicked fist.
> . . .
> Will you call this a fast,
>   a day acceptable to the LORD?
> Is not this the fast that I choose:
>   to loose the bonds of injustice,
>   to undo the thongs of the yoke,
> to let the oppressed go free,
>   and to break every yoke?
> Is it not to share your bread with the hungry,
>   and bring the homeless poor into your house;
> when you see the naked, to cover them,

and not to hide yourself from your own kin? (Isa 58:3–7).

The emphasis on God's concern for the poor continues in the New Testament. Consider these examples:

> [Jesus] looked up at his disciples and said: "Blessed are you who are poor, for yours is the kingdom of God" (Luke 6:20).

> Listen, my beloved brothers and sisters. Has not God chosen the poor in the world to be rich in faith and to be heirs of the kingdom that he has promised to those who love him? (Jas 2:5).

> Blessed are those who hunger and thirst for righteousness, for they will be filled (Matt 5:6).

The foregoing only samples the scores of verses or passages of Scripture that indicate God's "preferential option for the poor." Baptist ethicist Glen Stassen counts 1,060 occurrences of the Hebrew words *tsedeqa* (righteousness) and *mishpat* (justice) and the Greek word *dikaiosuné* (can be translated as either righteousness or justice) in the Bible. He expresses dismay at how little attention these themes get in many contemporary churches, compared to hot-button issues such as abortion or homosexuality, which appear very seldom or not at all in the pages of Scripture. Stassen calls this "kangaroo exegesis" because of our tendency to "hop over" those biblical concepts and mandates that we find threatening or that make us uncomfortable to get to those with which we find ourselves on safer ground despite their comparatively minuscule representation in the Bible.[13]

The affluence many of us in the global North enjoy tends to deaden us to the poverty and suffering of the global South. More insidiously, and of greater peril to our souls, our relative wealth (*obscene* wealth in comparison to much of the world) creates a dependence upon luxury. This dependence demands that we find or invent justifications for why we are wealthy and they are not, and why the status quo ought to remain in place. The postwar economic boom in the United States that lasted, with brief lapses, for six decades coincided during much of that span with the Cold War and its demonization of communism and glorification of capitalism. Even today, more than twenty years after the fall of the Berlin Wall and the collapse of the Soviet bloc, mere baseless accusations of socialism against political figures in the US can provoke a knee-jerk reaction of irrational fear and anger.

---

13. Stassen, "Christian Ethics."

Verbal Kint in the movie *The Usual Suspects* says, famously, "The greatest trick the devil ever pulled was convincing the world he didn't exist."[14] But the devil has more than one trick in his bag, and one he has used to great effect throughout American history has been to bind capitalism, religion, and patriotism in an unholy alliance, the mere questioning of which constitutes in many minds both treason and sacrilege. Many Americans have become so convinced of the inseparability of our economic-political system and our religious practices that to question free-market capitalism is tantamount to burning the American flag or desecrating a church. For some, it is virtually unthinkable, so deeply embedded this nefarious union has become in our collective unconscious.

Clearly, in such an environment, the idea of God's preferential option for the poor doesn't have much of a chance. That liberation theology first arose in Latin American countries where Marxism had also taken root constitutes another serious strike against it among many North American Christians. The cozy marriage of capitalism and Christianity in the US assures that any brand of theology (or anything else in the realm of ideas) arising in such a context will die a quick and ignominious death in certain churches on these shores. The preponderance of biblical evidence in support of this "preferential option" carries little weight when people associate it with an economic system and political ideology they have been conditioned to fear and despise.

Such is the case even, or perhaps especially, in those churches that proclaim most loudly and adamantly that they are "Bible-believing." This tendency signals the triumph of conventional political ideology and groupthink over serious and honest biblical interpretation—a triumph that has spread rapidly among both "red state" and "blue state" Christians in recent years. When the political party line, whether on the left or the right, dictates one's theology and the way one reads and interprets the Bible, rather than the other way around, beware. When politicians, pundits, and ideologues co-opt the church, the church loses its spiritual authority and forfeits its prophetic role in society.

We need to reclaim and proclaim God's preferential option for the poor, not as a theological innovation but as the most responsible reading of the Scriptures and the most faithful expression of discipleship. If discipleship means walking in the way of Jesus, then faithful discipleship means

14. "One Day in Turkey," *The Usual Suspects*, 1995.

siding with, advocating for, and seeking the empowerment and full flour-ishing of the world's poor.

As we will see, the Lord's Prayer—like the rest of the Sermon on the Mount (in Matthew); like the Sermon on the Plain (in Luke); and like most of Jesus's parables, sayings, and deeds of power (in all the gospels)—had as its intended audience people who were economically and socially margin-alized. In other words, poor. If Jesus cared enough about poor people to give them a model prayer; to spend the vast majority of his time teaching, healing, organizing, and living among them; and finally to die at the hands of the religio-political complex in large part because he championed their cause—if all this is true, should we not also express and live out a "prefer-ential option" for the poor?

We pray to our Father who aren't in heaven. Our Father who aren't lying in a hammock somewhere while God's people suffer. Our Father who *are* here among those people—the poor, persecuted, and marginal-ized ones—sharing their struggles, their sufferings, and their joys. Our Father who are calling us to join those poor ones in that difficult yet joyful struggle. Our Father who are on the side of the poor and are asking us to come over to that side too.

A DANGEROUS GOD: INCARNATION

In one of its most distinctive features, the Christian faith insists that God entered the world as a real human being at a particular point in history. The basic historical facts about Jesus of Nazareth are well-established. For instance, he was a Palestinian Jew who lived from approximately 4 BCE to 30 CE; he had an active mission from one to three years, mostly in the region around the Sea of Galilee; and he was executed on a Roman cross outside Jerusalem by order of the procurator Pontius Pilate. On the other hand, other claims that Christians make about Jesus cannot be verified by objective observation, scientific inquiry, or historical investigation. These include the claims that he in some way shared in the divine nature, that he was raised from the dead by the power of God, and that he will sit as Judge of all humanity at the consummation of history. That Jesus was simultane-ously fully human and fully divine, and that he is the second Person of the Trinity, are assertions of orthodox Christian faith that took five or six cen-turies to get hammered out by a series of church councils. Not all Christians hold these assertions to be true, and not all who accept them understand them the same way.

I do not intend to go into a detailed discussion of the ins and outs of these issues. For our purposes, let it suffice to say that the doctrine of the Incarnation ratifies the claim that God is not (and has no intention of being) locked away in a heavenly ghetto. Or in a tomb, for that matter. God is present and active in the world of creation and human affairs. The Incarnation puts God's stamp of approval on humanity and provides the strongest piece of evidence of God's deep concern for what happens to God's human creatures.

The first of the Bible's two accounts of creation, found in the first chapter of Genesis, begins with the creation of light on day one and culminates on the sixth day with God's creation of animals and people. Humanity's creation brings God's creative work to a crescendo, and it differs from the other acts of creation in two important ways.

First, Genesis 1:26 has God say, "Let us make humankind in our image, according to our likeness." No other creature of God's, whether sun or moon, plant or animal, bird of the air or fish of the sea, is said to have been created in God's image and likeness. There is something special, something unique about humankind and our relation to our Creator.

The second difference between the creation of humans and the creation of everything else comes when God assesses God's own work. After each of the first five days of creation, and the first part of day six, comes the refrain, "And God saw that it was good." After humanity comes on the scene, however, God looks at the world God has created and declares it to be "very good" (Gen 1:31). God's opinion of the created order is a positive one—it is good. But God's crowning work of creation is humankind. Our presence in the world causes God's approval to ratchet up a notch—with humans in it, the world is *very* good.

So we see that from the very beginning God has had a special place in God's heart for humanity. But humans were always separate from God—created in God's image but still other. Then came Jesus.

Mark wrote his gospel, the earliest of the four accounts of Jesus's life in the New Testament, around 70 CE. This shortest gospel begins with the preaching of John the Baptist and the adult Jesus's proclamation of the nearness of the reign of God. Although in the very first verse of his gospel he declares Jesus to be "the Son of God," Mark portrays Jesus as a thoroughly human figure, and gives no indication that he thinks of Jesus as God

Incarnate. In fact, in one scene Jesus indirectly denies having divine status. When approached by a rich man who greets him as "Good Teacher," probably in an attempt to flatter him and curry his favor, Jesus replies, "Why do you call me good? No one is good but God alone" (Mark 10:17–18).

One plainly sees the development of the tradition in the next two gospels, Matthew and Luke. These writers composed their works during the 80s and drew heavily upon Mark. A new feature that Mark had not included—the birth narrative—makes its appearance in these later gospels. Matthew and Luke, drawing upon different traditions, each tell a story of how Jesus's birth came about and the circumstances surrounding it. Despite the harmonizations that appear every Christmas in crèches and church plays, Luke's and Matthew's birth narratives are quite incompatible. Clearly, each Evangelist shaped the tradition he had inherited to conform to the theological points he wanted to make in his gospel as a whole. For our purposes, simply note that as time went on, people began paying more attention to Jesus's origins. Like other great heroes in the Greco-Roman world, Jesus needed a birth story demonstrating that his origins predicted his greatness, and Luke and Matthew obliged. Each in his own way showed that Jesus's credentials were of the highest order. Angels predicted his conception (both Matthew and Luke), his birth occasioned great political upheaval and turmoil (Matthew), and as an infant he had visitors suited to the respective Evangelists' theologies—Gentile magi bearing gifts fit for royalty (Matthew) and shepherds, representatives of the most marginalized people in Jewish society (Luke). These developments show that the churches in the latter decades of the first century had begun to think of Jesus in a new way.

By the time John, the last gospel in the New Testament, came along, probably in the 90s, the tradition had developed to such an extent that John could speak of Jesus as the Word, or Logos, who was coequal with God. The concept of the Logos came from Hellenistic philosophy, where it signified a sort of organizing principle for the universe. John borrowed this concept from the Greeks and combined it with the rich associations of *dabar*, Hebrew for "word," and applied both ideas to Jesus. "In the beginning was the Word [logos/dabar], and the Word was with God, and the Word was God," the fourth gospel begins.

"In the beginning," of course, echoes the language of creation in Genesis, and John employs that phrase quite deliberately to place Jesus (as the Word) with God before the beginning of the world. His readers would not have found this as shocking as one might expect, considering that a strand of tradition in the Bible imagines the figure of Wisdom present with God as a sort of co-creator.[15] John combines the Hebraic and Greek understandings when he refers to Jesus as the Word.

Things take an unexpected turn, however, in verse 14 of John 1, where we find this bold assertion: "The Word became flesh and lived among us, and we have seen his glory, the glory as of a father's only son, full of grace and truth." Here we find the most concisely expressed basis in the entire New Testament for what would come to be known as the doctrine of the Incarnation. John 1:14 stands as one of the watershed verses of the Bible. The Word, the creative principle of the universe who has shared in God's very being from all eternity, became flesh and lived among us. Here in a nutshell is the most distinctive teaching of the Christian faith. In some mysterious way we cannot fully understand, God entered the created world as a real flesh-and-blood human being.

At this point John parts company with both the Greeks and the Jews. Those who accepted Greek philosophy, especially the Platonic tradition, would have been appalled at the suggestion that a divine being would have "become flesh." For them, a harsh dualism separated spirit and flesh. Spirit partook of the world of pure forms, while flesh belonged to the evil world of shadows. The immortal spirit, or soul, had somehow got trapped in flesh— they sometimes referred to the body as the "prison house of the soul"—and its goal was to get free and return to the eternal world of pure forms.[16] People employed various means, including prayer, religious devotion, asceticism, and, paradoxically, hedonism, to free the soul of the confines of the flesh. For the Word, or Logos, to descend from the pure world of eternity and deliberately enter supposedly evil flesh sounded not only counterintuitive, even nonsensical, to these Greek thinkers, but also offensive and perverse.

15. See especially Proverbs 3:19–20 and 8:22–31. For an example of this theology from the deuterocanonical literature (books that appear in the Roman Catholic scriptural canon but are not considered authoritative by Protestants or Jews), see the book known as Wisdom of Solomon.

16. See Plato, *Phaedo*. Consider, for instance, these two quotes attributed to Socrates just before his execution: "The lovers of knowledge are conscious that the soul was simply fastened and glued to the body—until philosophy received her, she could only view real existence through the bars of a prison, not in and through herself;" and, "Those too who have been pre-eminent for holiness of life are released from this earthly prison, and go to their pure home which is above, and dwell in the purer earth; and of these, such as have duly purified themselves with philosophy live henceforth altogether without the body, in mansions fairer still which may not be described, and of which the time would fail me to tell."

The Jews in John's audience would not have had a problem with the "enfleshment" of the Word—Hebraic thought had always seen the created order and the body in a more positive light than the Greeks—but they would have had serious problems with other implications of the Word's enfleshment. Their beef would have been that the Word's becoming flesh abrogated the unity of God. The bedrock creed of Judaism then and now is the *Shema*: "Hear, O Israel: the LORD our God, the LORD is one" (Deut 6:4 TNIV). The enfleshment of the Word, whom John had already equated with God, troubled the monotheistic Hebraic mind profoundly. Other controversial statements in John, such as Jesus's claiming the divine name for himself in his series of "I Am" statements ("I am the Good Shepherd," "I am the Light of the World," etc.) and his assertion that "the Father and I are one" (John 10:30), did not help. For a human being to make such claims would have been deemed heretical in the extreme, and the angry reaction of "the Jews" in the gospel probably reflected fairly accurately the perspective of non-Christian Jews who read or heard these claims.[17]

On top of all this, John and the other Evangelists claimed that Jesus's ministry concluded not with a tranquil retirement or a natural death surrounded by his faithful disciples and friends, but with his excruciating death by one of the most inhumane means of execution ever devised: crucifixion.

The Romans did not invent crucifixion—they got it from the Persians—but, as they did with many other features they borrowed from other cultures, they perfected it. That is, if turning a simple configuration of wooden beams and a few nails or a coil of rope into a device of supreme torture and humiliation can be dignified with the word "perfected." The

---

17. The writer of the gospel of John was not anti-Semitic; he was, in fact, a Jew himself. But he wrote during a time (90–110 CE) when the conflict between Jews who accepted Jesus as the Messiah and those who did not was growing more and more severe. In hindsight, we know that the schism between the two groups, which continues to this day, had already begun by John's time. That break had already advanced to the point that John and his congregation had started to see themselves as separate from mainstream Judaism; thus, John's use of "the Jews" for Jesus's opponents in the gospel. Members of John's church found themselves in the midst of heated controversies with those Jews who did not share their convictions about Jesus, and as in many disputes among siblings, the language often became bitter and recriminating. To the world's extreme misfortune, subsequent generations of Christians who did not know the context in which John wrote took his depiction of "the Jews" at face value. After Christianity became the dominant faith in the Roman Empire and later in Europe, this animus toward Jewish people led to slander, persecution, and violence against them throughout Christendom. Anti-Semitism produced pogroms, forced exile, and, finally, the horrors of the Shoah. For a discussion of these issues, see Crossan, *Who Killed Jesus?*

authorities did not sentence Roman citizens or ordinary lawbreakers to crucifixion. Citizens who committed capital crimes were executed in a relatively quick and painless way; beheading was one common method. The law reserved crucifixion for slaves and enemies of the state—those who had dared to rise up against mighty Rome with seditious intent.

The Romans designed every feature of crucifixion, every step in the process, to cause maximum pain, humiliation, and horror on the part of not only the victim but the onlookers as well. To increase its value as a deterrent, they set up crosses in prominent places, such as hills overlooking a town or along busy roadways. The victim's death was on public display, and it was not a quick death. If the guards did not break his legs so that he could no longer push himself up to breathe, a reasonably healthy victim might linger for days. And as a final indignity, one that was especially hard for Jews to swallow, the Romans routinely refused to allow friends or family members to bury their crucified loved ones. That Pilate agreed to give Jesus's body to Joseph of Arimathea for burial, if this account from the gospels does indeed reflect historical reality, means that Jesus was one of the lucky few. Most of those who died on the cross remained there to be eaten by carrion birds, dogs, or other wild animals. As if this were not bad enough, in some cases the feasting may have begun before the victim was completely dead. Crucifixion was unmitigated horror from beginning to end.

For Jesus to have undergone this torturous, shameful death, and for his disciples, Paul, and later the four Evangelists still to insist that he was the long-expected Messiah, let alone the Son of God or the very incarnation of God in human flesh, must have sounded to their first-century hearers and readers utterly ludicrous. Nonsensical. An insult to God. For good reason Paul called the message of the cross "a stumbling block to Jews and foolishness to Gentiles" (1 Cor 1:23). For anyone to proclaim "Christ crucified," and to say it with *pride*, must have sounded like the ravings of a lunatic.

But the original disciples and later the writers of the New Testament made precisely this claim. Jesus, a Galilean peasant who had been sentenced by the duly appointed administrator of Roman law to a horrific, ignominious death by crucifixion, was actually the Christ.[18] The Son of God. The apocalyptic Son of Man. God-in-the-flesh.

---

18. *Christos* (Gk.) means "anointed one," and translates the Hebrew word *mashiyach*, or messiah.

This dramatic upheaval and overturning of expectations came about because of the utterly unexpected event of Jesus's resurrection. I say "unexpected" because, although all four gospels report that Jesus predicted both his death and his resurrection more than once in the hearing of his disciples, the raising of a single individual did not fit any existing understanding of resurrection. Those who believed in it expected a general resurrection of all people at the end of the age, as a prelude to the final judgment. One individual's resurrection apart from the rest of humankind was completely unanticipated. Knowing what we now do about the way the mind works—when we receive new information we try first to assimilate it into patterns of meaning we have already established; if that doesn't work, we often reject the new information entirely—it is not altogether surprising that Jesus's disciples would have failed to comprehend that Jesus was to be raised.

In fact, not everyone within first-century Judaism subscribed to the notion that there would be any kind of resurrection at all. Resurrection was still a relatively new concept in Jewish thought when Jesus came along. It had developed in the second century BCE, like a number of other innovations, such as synagogue worship; the belief in angels, demons, and an afterlife; and the development of parties or sects, such as the Pharisees and Sadducees. It was, in fact, the Pharisees who introduced or popularized many of these innovative beliefs. Contrary to what a lot of people think, the Pharisees were the theological liberals of their day. The other group, the Sadducees, were the staunch traditionalists. They did not accept the existence of angels, demons, resurrection, or any of the other new-fangled ideas the Pharisees had embraced so readily. *Too* readily, in the Sadducees' opinion. The Sadducees were so conservative that they still only accepted the Torah—the first five books of the Bible—as Scripture. The Pharisees, on the other hand, included the Prophets and at least some of the books categorized in the Hebrew Bible as the "Writings" (e.g., Psalms, Esther, and Daniel) in their canon of Scripture.

Because of Jesus's fierce confrontations with the Pharisees in the gospels, especially Matthew, many readers think of the Pharisees as conservative obstructionists who feared or resented Jesus's supposed innovations. Quite the opposite was the case. The Pharisees were pretty adept theological innovators themselves. In today's terms, they were the liberal mainline Protestants to the Sadducees' conservative evangelicals.

The pharisaical faction within Judaism arose in the latter half of the second century BCE, as did their expectation of a general resurrection at the end of the age. These developments came about at least partly due to the death of Jewish martyrs at the hands of the Syrian ruler of Palestine, Antiochus IV Epiphanes, and during the Maccabean revolt against his rule.[19]

Despite its eventual success, this revolt raised some thorny theological problems for the Jews. To that point, despite a few hints and suggestions scattered among the books of the Prophets and the Writings, the common understanding was that this life is the only life there is. They imagined an abode of the dead, *Sheol*, but only as a shadowy realm where the shades of the formerly alive had an impotent sort of semi-existence. One could hardly call it an afterlife; more of an afterdeath. In fact, the New International Version of the Bible consistently translates the term Sheol as simply "the grave." It was the common destination of all, bad and good alike.

Because they had no genuine concept of a meaningful life after death, the people of Israel understood judgment as a this-worldly phenomenon. Furthermore, they understood judgment primarily in corporate terms. If the nation or its rulers were unfaithful to their covenant with God, the whole nation would experience judgment and punishment. They used this corporate judgment model to categorize military defeats, plagues, and catastrophes such as the Babylonian Exile. The nation's sin was corporate, so the nation stood or fell together.

That thinking began to change with the persecution under Antiochus and the ensuing revolt. For the first time, at least on such a large scale, observant and obedient Jews were being killed. The rebellion had begun in response to abominable offenses Antiochus had perpetrated against Jewish sensibilities in an effort to eradicate Judaism and Hellenize the region. The rebels' cause was just, their hearts were true, and yet they were being killed. Brands of theology that blithely held that God rewards faithfulness and punishes apostasy, or could imagine only corporate judgments or blessings, no longer satisfied a growing number of people. They needed a new way of making sense of life and death.

---

19. In 176 BCE, Antiochus IV came to power as the Seleucid ruler of Syria, which at the time included Palestine. A staunch pagan, Antiochus quickly set in motion a program to Hellenize Judea. Among other offenses against Jewish sensibilities, he forbade circumcision and profaned the Temple by erecting an altar to Zeus and allowing the sacrifice of pigs. In response to these provocations, a band of Jewish rebels, led by a patriarchal figure named Matthias, rose up against Antiochus. One of Matthias's sons, Judas, earned the nickname *Maccabeus*, or "Hammer," for his ferocity in battle, thus giving the Maccabean revolt its name. For a full description of these events, see Josephus, *War*, 1.1.2–4.

That's when the resurrection concept began to gain traction, but they still expected it to be a corporate phenomenon. All would be raised together at the end of the age, but with the new twist that they would be judged on an individual basis. Some would be judged worthy of life and reward, and others worthy of death and punishment. Daniel 12:1–2, which probably comes from around the time of the Maccabean revolt, expresses the idea this way: "At that time your people shall be delivered, everyone who is found written in the book. Many of those who sleep in the dust of the earth shall awake, some to everlasting life, and some to shame and everlasting contempt." Corporate criteria still held sway—for the Jews, the covenant with God that found its fullest expression in the Torah; for the later Christian inheritors of the resurrection-and-judgment scenario, the "new covenant" Jesus inaugurated—but the criteria would be applied on a case-by-case basis. The writer of Revelation, for instance, uses the metaphor of whether one's name is written in the Lamb's book of life.

We can discern a movement away from corporate reward and punishment to this new emphasis on individual judgment in the writings of the prophets. Jeremiah declares a change in the way God looks at sin (or at least in the way humans assume God looks at sin) when he writes, "In those days they shall no longer say: 'The parents have eaten sour grapes, and the children's teeth are set on edge.' But all shall die for their own sins; the teeth of everyone who eats sour grapes shall be set on edge" (Jer 31:29–30).

By the time of Jesus, the Pharisees had become an influential minority in Jewish life, and their understanding and depiction of resurrection was becoming commonplace. The gospels give us no evidence that any of Jesus's disciples objected to his predictions of resurrection. But they still understood it the way the Pharisees did—as a general resurrection to take place just before the great judgment. Jesus really upset the applecart by being raised alone.

Of course, Jesus was, to say the least, a special case. He was the Son of God—the incarnation of the Holy One; the Ancient of Days in human flesh. And God's raising him clearly indicated both that God approved of the way he had lived his life and that God disapproved of the way the Romans and the Jewish aristocracy had conspired to put him to death.

I recognize that to say that Jesus was the incarnation of God, and that he died, and that God then raised him from the dead is enough to make one's head swim. How could God raise Jesus if Jesus was himself God? How could God be in two places at once, and simultaneously alive and dead?

The key is to remember that the designations of Jesus as Son of God, Word-made-flesh, Lord, God of God and Light of Light, and so on came about *after* Easter. In all likelihood, neither Jesus nor anyone else used these titles for him during his lifetime. We don't know who first applied these honorifics to Jesus, or when they did it, but it was surely only after much reflection on his life, his death, and the world-shattering event of his resurrection.

It was almost certainly the resurrection that prompted the earliest Christians to begin using these exalted titles for Jesus. Only after several centuries did the church work out how Jesus could have been God and human at the same time, and therefore how God could possibly have raised God from the dead. For our present purposes, we just need to grasp that Jesus is the fullest human expression there has ever been of who God is, and that his solo resurrection confirmed that assertion in a wholly unprecedented and unlooked-for way.

Paul understood that Jesus's resurrection, while utterly unique, still bore connections to the general resurrection everyone had come to expect. He called Jesus the "first fruits" of the resurrection, referring to the practice of taking the first yield of one's crop and offering it to God. The Hebrew people did this to express their gratitude and declare their trust that the one who had provided these first fruits would in turn provide the whole crop. Jesus, by this way of thinking, was raised not just as an isolated miracle, but as God's pledge that the general resurrection would follow. Paul expected it to follow within his lifetime. We know that didn't happen, but the promise remains valid. Regardless of the length of the interval, Jesus's resurrection guarantees our own resurrection.

To state the obvious, if God had not been incarnated in Jesus—if the Word had not "become flesh and lived among us"—none of this would have been possible. If God had been content to lie in the divine hammock, we would have no assurance of resurrection and eternal life. But God left the heaven ghetto and entered the grit and grime of the world. We—all humanity—are the beneficiaries of this extraordinary largesse.

REMOVING THE OPPOSITION

A bit of personal history. I grew up and lived my first twenty-two years in a small town in the Midwest where the primary industry was the mining of high-sulfur coal and our chief products were humidity and mosquitos. It was and is a blue-collar area, and I am the son of a proud union man.

As a child I attended the First Baptist Church in this small town. In addition to being blue-collar, my hometown—the whole region, really—was socially, politically, and, at least in the circles in which I moved, theologically conservative, bordering on fundamentalist. My church fit this mold. By far the largest Baptist church in the town and one of the largest in that section of my home state, it stood solidly in line with the conservative wing of the Southern Baptist Convention.

Perhaps it was a kinder, gentler time, or else my juvenile perspective did not catch all the nuances, but our church never seemed angry the way so many conservative evangelical churches do today. From my mother, who still lives in my hometown and still attends this church, I get the impression that they also have taken sides in the "culture wars" in the last decade or so. But I don't remember that element of shrillness or stridency that now characterizes so much of the evangelical world in the church of my youth. If anything, we were apolitical. Churches ought to be in the business of "winning souls," the thinking ran, not engaging in political maneuvering or public debates with the dreaded secular humanists.

Evangelism characterized the church in which I grew up. Every worship service featured an "invitation" for persons to renounce their sinful ways and accept Jesus Christ as their personal Savior. Many, if not most, sermons had an evangelistic orientation. The three or four pastors who served there during my childhood and teen years all played variations on a common theme: our need for salvation. The man who pastored the church when I was in grade school (needless to say, they were *all* men) used to talk about the struggle, the tug-of-war between God and the devil going on inside someone's soul. To my young mind he seemed a prophet or a mind-reader, because that described precisely how I felt inside (possibly due to the power of suggestion), and one Sunday at the age of nine, without giving anyone, including my parents, any forewarning, I "went forward" and prayed to have my sins forgiven and to invite Jesus into my heart. Not long after this highly emotional experience, I was baptized.

Now an official member of the church, I became very serious about trying to live the life God wanted me to. I can't say that this resolution made much difference when it came to getting along with my older brother or reforming my basically ornery nature, but when it came to church and other "God stuff," I jumped in with both feet. When I was in junior high, a two-year period that was in many ways pure hell for me, I took part in Sunday School and youth group activities with gusto. I prayed every night before bed, I attended retreats and other "spiritual" events, and I read the Bible from cover to cover. At some point during seventh grade, I began to feel a certain stirring that my pastor (and the whole tradition to which I belonged) put a name to: God was calling me into ministry.

My high school and early college years saw me reject a lot of what I had grown up believing, but the summer before I turned twenty I got turned back around. Through the influence of some supportive friends and what I believe was a mystical encounter with God, I became convinced that God still loved me and was calling me back into fellowship. I felt a reconfirmation of my earlier sense of a calling to vocational ministry.

Throughout all this time, I never questioned the basic narrative I had absorbed in my formative years. Even during my four or five years "in the wilderness," I didn't doubt the validity of that narrative. I was pretty sure I didn't believe it anymore, but it never occurred to me that I could reject a particular way of understanding God and the Christian faith without chucking the whole thing—baby, bathwater, and all.

That narrative—that way of framing the human predicament and God's solution to it—was pretty simple. That was and is a large part of its appeal. It is simple and it lends itself to quick, easy-to-comprehend communication. One could presumably make the presentation to a stranger in an elevator and could walk that person through the various steps and have her pray "the sinner's prayer" and "be saved" by the time the elevator reached her floor. It was so neat and pre-packaged. The steps involved could be made into little comic strips to hand out to people on the street or printed on a piece of paper the size of a business card and left in a public place, such as the men's room at a rest stop on the Interstate. The potential existed for a heathen to get off the highway to pee and get back in his car a sanctified Christian. Urinal evangelism. You never know—God works in mysterious ways, after all.

As the first step in this salvation process, you must admit you are a sinner. Second, you have to acknowledge that your sin creates an insurmountable barrier between you and a holy God. Third, you must believe that God sent Jesus, the Son of God, to break down that barrier through his death on the cross. In the fourth and final step, you confess your sins and receive the forgiveness that is *only* available through Jesus's blood. You must believe in the efficacy of Jesus's sacrifice for you and invite him into your heart.

It's just that easy.

Guided by my pastor, I followed this basic formula when I became a Christian, and countless others have followed this process or something like it to begin their own Christian journeys. I believe that my experience of salvation at age nine was genuine, and I have no reason to doubt that the vast majority of those who have traveled a similar route really did "receive Christ," whatever that may mean to those involved. God can use even our oversimplifications and slick product packaging to bring persons into communion with God. I would not hesitate to add my "amen" to that.

Having said that, however, I do believe this presentation of the gospel has serious flaws. God can certainly save someone through a flawed process, but it is equally certain that God doesn't want that person to remain bound to that inadequate understanding for life.

The problems begin to come to light when we delve a little deeper into the narrative. Our sin creates a barrier between us and God. Fair enough, but why? Because God is holy—the prophet Habakkuk describes God as too pure even to look upon sin or evil (Hab 1:13). That proof-text, along with God's demand that we be holy as God is holy, makes for a pretty insoluble problem.

We can't solve it, anyway. We are sinful by nature, so everything we touch becomes soiled by the corruption we carry about with us wherever we go. As Isaiah declares, even our *righteous* acts appear to God as filthy rags (Isa 64:6). The problem gets compounded further when we consider that God's commitment to justice (in this case, retributive or punitive justice) will not allow God simply to forgive our sins. We can't just get off scot-free, the argument runs, because that wouldn't be fair—it wouldn't satisfy God's sense of aggrieved justice. We (or a suitable substitute) must be punished. Because of the gravity of our offense, the only acceptable punishment is death. This explains the practice of animal sacrifice in the Old Testament. Instead of striking the Israelites dead when they sinned, God graciously allowed them to slaughter an innocent animal in their place. But the need to keep making the sacrifices over and over revealed this to be an imperfect system. The writer of the New Testament Epistle to the Hebrews, speaking of this sacrificial system, writes, "It is impossible for the blood of bulls and goats to take away sin [permanently]" (Heb 10:4). If it could, one sacrifice would be enough. That they had to keep killing those animals again and again and again demonstrated that a different solution to the sin problem had to be found.

So we have a situation in which we have built a wall of sin between us and God. It's too high for us to climb over, and everything we do, even something good and righteous, only serves to add more bricks to the wall. The bright idea of shedding the innocent blood of sheep and goats in place of our guilty blood quickly dims when we realize that these sacrifices only slow, or at best pause, the construction of the separation barrier. They do nothing to *remove* any bricks. From our side of the wall, the situation looks utterly hopeless.

Enter Jesus.

Because Jesus came in human flesh as the incarnation of God and led a sinless life of moral perfection, he is qualified to offer a sacrifice holy and perfect enough to remove the barrier once and for all. That's the primary reason for the Incarnation, according to this narrative: Jesus has to represent both parties in this legal conflict. He can represent the injured party, God, because he shares in a fundamental way the very nature of God. But he can at the same time, by virtue of his human flesh, represent the defendants in the case—namely, all of sinful humanity. He shares our nature but not our sin. He shares God's nature but not, apparently, God's thirst for vengeance or fierce commitment to retribution.

He does, however, accept the foregoing description of the human "sin predicament." So much so that he willingly offers his own life—his own blood—to take away our sin, appease God, and break down the barrier that separates us from God. Jesus can offer that perfect sacrifice that we ordinary humans have never been able to locate either in ourselves or in our substitutionary livestock. He can and does offer a once-for-all sacrifice that does away with the need for burnt offerings and other priestly efforts to appease God.

Except that it doesn't seem to be as once-for-all as it appears at first. Sure, Jesus only had to die once, but each individual—and that word *individual* is crucial—must apply Jesus's death to his own sins or else remain subject to God's wrath and *eternal* punishment in the fires of hell. God just can't seem to let it go. Until one invites Jesus into one's heart and believes in Jesus's sacrifice as the only means of salvation—until one is, in a rather gory metaphor, washed in Jesus's blood—God sees one as still hopelessly steeped in sin. As soon as one does undergo that bloodbath (so to speak), God puts on "Jesus glasses" that cause God to see Jesus when God looks at the newly redeemed Christian. That's what Paul means when he says that we "put on" Christ (Rom 13:14).

All this sounds kind of comical when you look at it in a certain way, but I find nothing comical about how this theory interprets what happened on the cross.

Because Jesus must take our sins upon himself and be put to death to make our forgiveness possible, this substitutionary theory says that as Jesus is raised up on the cross, God dumps on him all the sins of every person who has ever drawn breath or will do so in the future. Then, in a shocking turn of events, because God's eyes are too pure to look upon sin, God turns God's back on Jesus. For the first time ever, in his life on earth or in his eternally preexistent state as a member of the Trinity, Jesus experiences a break in his communion with God. At his lowest, most vulnerable point, as he feels the crushing effects of sin for the first time ever, God abandons him. Turns away. Walks out. Proponents of this view say that this explains Jesus's anguished cry of dereliction, "My God, my God, why have you forsaken me?" (Mark 15:34).

This is abhorrent theology. Not only does it paint God as a cold, calculating, inflexible, abusive parent, but it also neglects the profound truth Paul expresses in 2 Corinthians 5:19, that "God was *in Christ*, reconciling the world to himself" (NLT, emphasis added). It sets up an opposition between the Father and the Son.

A much healthier way to think of the interaction between God and Jesus at the cross sees God as being intimately involved with every part of the crucifixion—not as a puppet master orchestrating the action, but as an anguished parent suffering along with a beloved child. Not the stern, judging God who demands reparations before agreeing to dole out forgiveness. Not the meticulous bean-counter God who maintains a spreadsheet of everyone's sins and demands that each of them be accounted for before the books can be closed. Rather, this suffering God endures every moment of Jesus's agony along with him, weeps for this victim of imperial injustice, and stands in solidarity with him and with all who suffer. The cross becomes the paradigmatic symbol of God's deep connection with and love for this broken world. The shadow of the cross stretches not only over Golgotha in the first century, but over plague-ravaged Europe in the Middle Ages; over Salem, Massachusetts, in the 1600s; over Wounded Knee and the Trail of Tears; over the gates of Auschwitz and Dachau; over Dresden, Hiroshima, and Nagasaki; over Srebrenica, Kigali, and Darfur; over the scenes of wasting disease and starvation in Haiti, Ethiopia, and Somalia; over the beds where the victims of AIDS slowly succumb, very often dying alone and afraid. In short, the cross of Jesus stands in the midst of every scene of unjust suffering the world has ever known or will ever know. God is there, too, prostrate with grief, weeping and ululating and ensuring that no one in any of these scenes really dies alone or unnoticed.

God's hammock lies empty. The heaven ghetto has gone uninhabited. God was in Christ. God is in all those others. God is here.

Our Father who aren't in heaven.

2

Making It Holy, Keeping It Holy

. . . hallowed be thy name.

IF THE LORD'S PRAYER begins in an archaic and apparently ungrammatical way, "Our Father who art in heaven," the next line doesn't represent a marked improvement: "Hallowed be thy name." First of all, "hallowed" has been out of circulation for quite some time. It may have been common parlance four hundred years ago in Jacobin England, but it's a head-scratcher for most people today.

Second, the ambiguous structure of the sentence presents a problem. Hallowed be thy name. Putting the subject at the end of the sentence that way has not been in vogue since the days of Wordsworth or Shelley, and grammarians probably frowned on it even then.

We find a more significant difficulty than the awkward arrangement of the words, however, when we consider how to read the sentence. Is the mood simply indicative: "Thy name is hallowed"? Or does it carry a more subtle nuance of meaning, as in "Let thy name be hallowed," or, more expansively, "Let it be known to all that thy name is or should be hallowed"? Or is it a petition that carries the force of an imperative: "Hallow thy name" or "Make thy name hallowed"? This seemingly simple clause raises a lot of questions.

Let us now turn to these four important but perplexing words.

WHAT THE HECK IS HALLOWED?

"Hallowed" means holy. We most often encounter a form of this word today in "Halloween," which is a shortened form of "Hallow's Even," or "All Hallow's Eve." Halloween falls on October 31. The next day, November 1, is the church feast known as All Saints' Day or, in a more archaic form, All Hallows' Day.

So "Hallows" means "Saints." Now we're getting somewhere. Both "hallows" and "saints" translate the Greek word *hagioi*, which means "holy ones" or "ones set apart." We run across this word in the New Testament, most frequently in the letters of Paul and of those later authors who wrote in Paul's name. Paul often addressed his epistles to "the hagioi who are in (or at)" Philippi, Corinth, Rome, and so on. But what did he mean by that, and how does that inform our understanding of the petition, "Hallowed be thy name?"

Whatever else he may have meant, Paul probably considered the people to whom he was writing to be *holy*. Of course, he undoubtedly had a different idea of what constituted holiness than we do. In fact, the concept of holiness that we find throughout both testaments of the Bible differs a great deal from the common understanding of holiness today.

When many of us hear the word "holy," we tend to think of religious ritual or moral purity, and our thoughts along these lines tend not to be complimentary. "Holier than thou" is an epithet we reserve for those we consider self-righteous and hypocritical. Holiness's companion word, "saint," likewise suffers from its association with dry religion and moralism. It often amounts to little more than "goody-two-shoes" in the popular imagination. "I'd rather laugh with the sinners than cry with the saints," Billy Joel declares, because "the sinners are much more fun."[1] We know precisely what he means. Most people cannot even imagine a laughing, boisterous, earthy saint.

The church's veneration of saints and martyrs, a process that has been going on for nearly two millennia, sets up another obstacle to our getting back to the biblical understanding of holiness and sainthood. The Roman Catholic Church has led the way in this effort, with their elaborate calendar of feast days and strict criteria for canonization, but Christians of every stripe have engaged in this practice at one time or another. Even without a systematic process, we have a way of identifying Christians we admire and

---

1. Joel, "Only the Good Die Young."

letting our admiration drift over into the realm of veneration. For many, Martin Luther King Jr. and Mother Teresa are unofficial saints. Others look to John Wesley or Billy Graham. My own list of saints would include King, Oscar Romero, Desmond Tutu, Dorothy Day, and Dietrich Bonhoeffer.

There is something very natural and human about all this. We have a seemingly innate need for heroes. What Rocky Balboa does for us cinematically, what Ronald Reagan or Hillary Clinton (depending on our ideological leanings) does for us politically, what Michael Jordan and Mia Hamm do for us in the world of sports, King and Graham and others do for us spiritually: they serve as paragons for us to emulate. They broaden our horizons; they expand our definition of what is possible; sometimes they challenge or even alter our notions of what is good and true and desirable. In short, they serve as heroes. This is natural and even healthy, as long as our hero admiration doesn't devolve into hero worship.

But even if we don't fall into the trap of idolatry, another, more insidious danger lurks in this popular definition of sainthood: the danger of creating a hierarchy of spirituality. It is all too easy to create a multi-tiered "class system" in the life of the spirit. There are saints and then there are the rest of us. How can little old me possibly compare myself with someone as spiritually evolved as Francis of Assisi or Teresa of Calcutta? They are on a wholly other plane . . . and they are riding in first class. (Actually, Mother Teresa would probably be riding in coach; she would have exchanged her first class ticket and given the money to the poor.)

The danger in this is the relief we may feel when we contemplate these distinctions. There must have been something about these people—some holiness gene—that we simply lack. We're talking about spiritual giants here; I'm no Albert Schweitzer, after all, and that *lets me off the hook*. Saints like these can do the heavy lifting; surely God understands my limitations and has something less strenuous in mind for me. Saints are kind of like the Scrubbing Bubbles in those old bathroom cleaner commercials: "We work hard so you don't have to."

We see something like this in the history of interpretation of the Sermon on the Mount. This collection of Jesus's teachings spans three chapters in the gospel of Matthew and includes, among other things, the commands to "love your enemies" and "be perfect . . . as your heavenly Father is perfect" (Matt 5:48); the admonition, "Judge not lest ye be judged" (Matt 7:1 KJV); and the Lord's Prayer. We have no reason not to believe that Jesus meant for his hearers to take him seriously and thought them capable of carrying out his instructions. But over time, priests and teachers and biblical interpreters, whether sincere or self-serving, introduced the idea that Jesus did not mean for the Sermon to apply to *everyone*, rather only to a few select spiritual athletes. The rest of us could take a more allegorized approach to the Sermon and leave the literal or more strenuous application of its teachings to the priests, monks, nuns, and zealots who constituted the elect.

I consider myself to be a pretty ecumenically minded kind of guy, but from time to time my Baptist prejudices and predilections get the better of me. This happens, for instance, when the subject of the clergy and laity comes up. I come from a congregationalist tradition that places great value on the priesthood of every believer and an idea bearing the curious moniker of "soul competence." Baptists see each person (in more antiquated language, each "soul") as competent to approach God with no mediator besides Jesus Christ and no advocate apart from the Holy Spirit. Everyone has equal access to God. Everyone is competent to enter into a relationship with the Divine Center. We have no need of a special class of priests and mediators ("clergy"), since all of us (the "laity") have equal competence.

Jesus did not mean for only a special few to take him and his message seriously, nor was he in the habit of spouting airy nonsense that had no bearing on life in the real world. A practical person, he had practical concerns and a practical approach to creating a new community that could transform the world in important, practical ways. When he said, "Love your enemies," he was not setting forth some unattainable ideal that everyone could applaud and ignore; he meant for us to love our enemies. Glen Stassen has exploded the notion that the Sermon on the Mount's teachings are impracticable and has offered a reading that highlights their pragmatism and concrete attainability.[2] Jesus does not reserve the Sermon, the Prayer, and his other teachings for a spiritual elite or a professional class of Christians. He gives them to everybody.

Here we find the necessary corollary to the concept of soul competence: if we all have equal *access* to God and equal *competence* to form a relationship of trust and obedience with God, then we all bear equal *responsibility* to do so. Ah, there's the rub. When you put it that way, having clergy or saints to do the work so we don't have to starts to sound pretty good.

---

2. Stassen, *Just Peacemaking*, 33–51.

But we need to reject that sort of spiritual abdication vigorously. Peril lies in wait for us when we deny our competence and opt out of our responsibility. Secondhand Christianity endangers one's soul.

Which brings us back to Paul and his emulators, and what they mean by hagioi, or saints. As I noted in passing above, besides "saints" or "holy ones," one can also translate hagioi as "those who are set apart." That gets to the heart of what the biblical writers of both testaments mean when they speak of holiness. A person or object becomes holy when set apart for a special purpose. For example, God sets apart the Aaronic priests for the purpose of bringing sacrifices, offering prayers, and in various other ways mediating between the community of Israel and God. Even a cursory glance at the myriad purity regulations in the Hebrew Scriptures will demonstrate that it was this "set-apartness" of Aaron and his descendants—of the whole tribe of Levi, in fact—that necessitated their removal from the day-to-day life of the community. They went to very particular and meticulous (sometimes to the point of being comical) lengths to preserve this set-apartness and protect their purity. Contact with corpses, sick people, even menstruating women, was thought to make a person unclean and therefore unfit for service before a holy God, so it was in their interest to stay above the fray, as it were. Physical separation reflected their spiritual set-apartness. So when Paul applies the concept of holiness to his readers, he means that, just like the priests and Levites of the old days, they are to consider themselves holy—set apart for a purpose.

This idea does not originate with Paul; he simply extends to the church the declaration God makes about the entire nation of Israel while they are encamped at the foot of Mount Sinai. God says, "You shall be for me a priestly kingdom and a holy nation" (Exod 19:6). God sets apart *all* the people, not just the priests. Paul (and later Peter, who makes it even more explicit—see 1 Peter 2:9) merely updates this promise to suit the new circumstances.

The surprising innovation in Paul's use of the term for his congregations only appears when we consider the makeup of those congregations. Paul was famous—or infamous, if you were to ask his detractors—for declaring that God has opened the path to salvation through Christ to everybody. And I mean *everybody*. Not just men, but women as well. Not just the rich, but the poor as well. Not just the freeborn, but slaves as well. And, in what was at the time the most radical and controversial claim of all, Paul said grace is open not just to the Jew, but to the Gentile as well. We're not talking about upstanding, monotheistic, God-fearing, quasi-Jewish Gentiles like Peter's friend Cornelius, either. We're talking about flat-out pagans. Paul says that anyone who hears the good news about Jesus can receive salvation, and that everyone who responds to that call in faith should be considered holy, set apart.

In one of the absolute high-water marks in Scripture, and in all of Christian thought down to this day, Paul expresses this sublime idea in sublime language: "There is no longer Jew or Greek, there is no longer slave or free, there is no longer male and female, for all of you are one in Christ Jesus" (Gal 3:28). Saints aplenty. All set apart. All called out. All holy. Hallowed.

HALLOWED, NOT HOLLOW

In the Lord's Prayer, we declare God's name to be hallowed, or ask for it to be hallowed, or volunteer to make it hallowed, or perhaps all of the above. But you would hardly guess from our culture that tens of millions of people in this country alone recite this Prayer every week. In contemporary America, the hallowing of God's name does not seem to be a high priority. Every day we see and hear people abuse, misuse, co-opt, trivialize, and in scores of other ways empty God's name of all meaning. The ubiquitous "OMG" is bad enough, but now we see with some regularity "OMFG." Really? OMFG? Have we no reverence for anything or anyone, even *God*, anymore? It indicates yet again that in our day, we more often consider God's name hollow than hallowed.

I am using "name" here in its most literal sense. Later in this chapter I will take a look at what it means to make God's name hallowed in the sense that "name" is often used in Scripture, as shorthand for God's character, power, and being. For now, though, let's just look at God's name.

The Third Commandment reads, "You shall not take the name of the Lord your God in vain" (Exod 20:7 ESV). When I was growing up, preachers and Sunday School teachers commonly interpreted this to mean that we should not use the words "God," "Jesus," or "Christ" as curse words. This commandment has a much more profound meaning than that, and later we will explore both that meaning and the relationship between the Commandment and the Lord's Prayer. But even if taking the Lord's name in vain means more than, "Watch your language, young man," it certainly does not mean less than this. In fact, the cavalier use of the literal name of God serves as a leading indicator of the low esteem in which many hold God's name in the broader sense of God's character and intention for the world.

As a sometime preacher and poet, I have a curious relationship with words. On one hand, I believe passionately in the power of words to inspire, to illuminate, and to catalyze change—both for good and for evil. Martin Luther King Jr. used the power of words to motivate a people to love courageously in the face of hate, and ultimately helped make America a more free and just place for all. Adolf Hitler used the power of words to stoke militant hatred and fear, which ultimately led to unimaginable horror for millions.

On the other hand, I think it important to demystify words whenever possible. It seems odd to me that certain combinations of syllables and vocal sounds should be considered inherently wrong or sinful. I sometimes deliberately say certain words that shock people, not for some perverse pleasure in offending someone, but to try to cut through the word to the idea behind the word—to bring it out into the open so it can be addressed. Words are so often used to obfuscate, to deflect, to manipulate, that I feel it almost a duty to pull back the curtains of respectability and decorum from time to time. I want to find what lurks in the shadows behind the words or the avoidance of certain words and try to drag it out into the light. Using the "N-word" is an obvious indicator of bigotry. But scrupulously avoiding racial slurs and feigning outrage at their use, while all the time keeping quiet about the many ways one benefits from a society founded on racism, is hypocritical at best. This hinders rather than advances the struggle for true racial justice, equality, and reconciliation.

One way to recognize the power of words to shape attitudes and actions is to use inclusive language whenever possible. To some people this seems trivial, and in certain quarters we see a backlash against what is pejoratively called political correctness. But it's not trivial at all. To use a simple example, consider the words "fireman" and "firefighter." Imagine you are bringing up a young child, boy or girl, and you don't want to impel him or her to adopt stereotyped gender roles. You want to raise the child to be respectful, responsible, and committed to equality and fairness. Now imagine that every time you talk about a person who puts out fires for a living (and young kids of both sexes seem fascinated by this occupation), you use the word "fireman." Likewise with "policeman," "Congressman," and so on. Over time, the child will get the message that some jobs are just for boys and others are just for girls ("nurse" and "stewardess" come to mind)—precisely the opposite of what you wanted to convey. That's how enculturation happens, and the words we use make a strong contribution to that process.

There is an enormous difference, however, between favoring certain words over others for the purpose of fostering respect and openness to the broadest horizon of possibility, and doing so in order to *appear* respectful and not to offend. Around the time of Barack Obama's first inauguration in 2009, pundits, commentators, and average folks all over the country said all the right things about the progress we had made as a nation in electing a black President. The succeeding six years, however, have seen us become more polarized politically, economically, and ideologically than at any other time in recent memory. A great many of the divisions have had racial overtones, as well. Immigration, health care, capital punishment, poverty and social services, even the trumped-up (pun intended) "birther" controversy—over and over we have found ourselves taking sides along class and racial lines.

Not that many people have had the courage to come right out and say it. President Jimmy Carter was roundly criticized for saying he saw an element of racism in the virulent opposition Obama faced over health care reform and other issues. Carter called it like he saw it and got shouted down. As long as no one burned a cross in someone's yard or pronounced a certain racial epithet, many Americans seemed content to pretend we didn't have a seven-ton elephant standing smack in the middle of our cocktail party. All those fine-sounding words started to ring a little hollow.

In the Lord's Prayer, Jesus calls upon us to see that God's name is hallowed. But if we do not couple our pious language with compassionate and concrete acts of justice, our words will ring hollow as well.

TAKING THE NAME IN VAIN

Taking God's name in vain means more, of course, than speaking the literal name of God in an inappropriate way. In the Bible, God's name stands as proxy for God's identity and character. When Moses asks for God's name, God replies, "I Am Who I Am," which seems at first blush an evasion, a non-answer. Shorthand for, "Who do you think you are, Buster? My name is none of your business." But perhaps the very circularity of the answer provides the clue we need to grasp the role of God's name in representing

God's character. Most obviously, "I Am Who I Am" connotes *being*. God is the One who is. Or, more simply, God is.

One of the more obscure theological terms one runs across in speaking of God's nature is *aseity*, which means "non-contingent being." It is technically improper to say that God *exists*, because existence carries with it the aroma of contingency. *We* exist. Animals and plants and rocks and oceans exist. The planets and stars and galaxies and nebulae exist. The entire universe, from the tiniest quarks and gluons to the farthest mind-boggling reaches of space, exists because another force brought it into being. Creation demands a Creator; being demands a Source, or as Paul Tillich put it, a Ground of Being. You, I, and the rest of creation have contingent being—we rely on a Source outside ourselves for our existence. God, on the other hand, simply *is*. Aseity says that God depends on no other power or source for God's being, God's *is-ness*. So when God declares God's name to be "I Am Who I Am," we're catching a glimpse of that is-ness. God's name points to God's nature and identity.

At a deeper level, though, "I Am Who I Am" points to more than being; it proclaims God's absolute freedom. We can alternatively translate the name as "I Will Be What I Will Be," and the future orientation hints even more strongly of the notion of freedom. As we saw above in the story of Peter and Cornelius, God remains entirely free to act as God chooses in every circumstance. No constraints exist apart from God's own self-restraint.

This is not an entirely comforting thought. If God always acts in complete freedom, how can one ever be certain where one stands with God? How does one know that God will not someday just fly off the handle and wipe one from the face of the earth?

We can never have absolute certainty, of course, but we can have supreme confidence, because God has proven supremely trustworthy. When we think and speak about God, we must always remember and hold in tension two words: *mystery* and *grace*. We have no access to God's inner life and ultimate nature. Mystery. But God always relates to us and the rest of creation in steadfast love. Grace. We can have confidence in God because God has proven, and still proves, faithful and gracious. In another part of Exodus, God again declares God's name to Moses, this time saying, "The LORD, the LORD, a God merciful and gracious, slow to anger, and abounding in steadfast love and faithfulness, keeping steadfast love for the thousandth generation, forgiving iniquity and transgression and sin, yet by no means clearing the guilty, but visiting the iniquity of the parents upon the children and the children's children, to the third and the fourth generation" (Exod 34:6–7). God's very name declares God's faithfulness—in grace and mercy, but also in discipline. That should give us both hope and pause.

In the Bible, names often have some significance in relation to the persons who bear them. Names can even be revelatory of character. A baby comes out of the womb gripping his twin brother's heel, and his parents name him Jacob, which literally means "heel grabber" but also has the figurative sense of "deceiver." This proves an entirely appropriate name for Jacob, who deceives people left and right his whole life long. His brother Esau, his father Isaac, his Uncle Laban, Esau again—all fall victim to Jacob's propensity for heel-grabbing. His name reveals his character.

That's why we should pay close attention to name changes in the Bible. Not every birth name hits its target as squarely as Jacob's does, but when someone receives a new name—especially if God does the re-naming—a revelation of character or role or destiny always comes as part of the bargain. Abram becomes Abraham, "father of a multitude," when God wishes to reinforce the promise of many descendants. The apostles give Joseph the name Barnabas, "Son of Encouragement," in recognition of his encouraging, selfless action in selling a piece of land and giving the proceeds to the church. Sometimes the new name is more aspirational or prophetic than descriptive. Jesus gives the impetuous and unreliable Simon the name Peter, or "the Rock," accurately predicting the way he would rebound from some notable failures to become rock-steady in his commitment to Christ and his leadership of the church. Even Jacob the heel-grabber gets a new name. After his all-night wrestling match at the ford of the Jabbok, his mysterious opponent gives him the name Israel, because he has "striven with God and with humans, and [has] prevailed" (Gen 32:28). Again, the renaming proves prophetic, for in the subsequent history of Jacob/Israel's descendants, the *nation* of Israel, struggling or wrestling with God remains a persistent theme.

If human name changes are significant in what they say about the person's character or destiny, how much more revelatory would a name change for *God* be? In the sixth chapter of Exodus—just three chapters after

Moses's encounter at the burning bush, when God declares, "I Am Who I
Am," and introduces the name YHWH[3] for the first time—God says this
to Moses:

> I am the LORD [YHWH]. I appeared to Abraham, Isaac, and Ja-
> cob as God Almighty, but by my name "the LORD" I did not make
> myself known to them. I also established my covenant with them,
> to give them the land of Canaan, the land in which they resided
> as aliens. I have also heard the groaning of the Israelites whom
> the Egyptians are holding as slaves, and I have remembered my
> covenant. Say therefore to the Israelites, "I am the LORD, and I will
> free you from the burdens of the Egyptians and deliver you from
> slavery to them. I will redeem you with an outstretched arm and
> with mighty acts of judgment (Exod 6:2–6).

Notice that in both this passage and the burning bush episode, God's
determination to free the Israelites from bondage provides the context.
God Almighty creates, protects, makes covenants, and keeps promises.
But when God comes as a Savior and Redeemer, as the God who hears
the groaning of an oppressed people and resolves to liberate them, God
declares a new name: YHWH. The name of God is revelatory. It discloses
God's character as the One who hears, who cares, and who delivers.

When we look at it that way, the idea of taking God's name in vain
takes on a whole new meaning. It means to claim to worship and serve
God while failing to share God's passion for justice and liberation. It means
to pledge allegiance to God without taking on the character of God and
expressing that character through actions of compassion and deliverance.
It means to want God but to have nothing to do with the reign of God. To
practice empty piety that fronts a heart full of self-centeredness, greed, apa-
thy, or hate is to take the name of God in vain. To claim to follow the God
of deliverance or God's Son Jesus—whose name incidentally means "God
saves"[4]—without doing what Glen Stassen and David Gushee call "deeds of

---

3. Many modern translations of the Hebrew Scriptures use "the LORD," written in
small capital letters, to signify that the word being translated is YHWH, the divine name
the scribes considered so holy that they would not pronounce it, and so never gave it
vowel points. "Jehovah" and "Yahweh" are two familiar attempts to make YHWH pro-
nounceable in English. To this day, when devout readers of the Hebrew Scriptures encounter YHWH in the text, they substitute the word *Adonai* for it. Adonai means "Lord;"
thus the use of LORD to translate YHWH, with the small capital letters to distinguish it
from a translation of the actual word "Adonai," which also appears frequently in the text.

4. Technically, "Jesus" is the Greek transliteration of the Hebrew name "Yeshua," or
"Yehoshua," which means "YHWH saves."

deliverance"[5] oneself is to take the name of God in vain. Nothing could be more vain, in the sense of empty, useless, or worthless, than that.

The Lord's Prayer, far from being an innocuous mantra we repeat by rote and then move on to other things, is a stirring call to arms. Not arms of war, but arms of compassion and healing and steadfastness in the face of evil. We need to be very careful, lest God should take us seriously and hold us to the commitments we make in the Prayer. To say, "Hallowed be thy name," becomes a dangerous undertaking when we begin to grasp that praying for God's name to be hallowed actually means, "Give me your character and set me loose in the world to carry out the deeds of justice, deliverance, and inclusive love that reflect that character."

Anything less would be to take the hallowed name of God in vain.

5. Stassen and Gushee, *Kingdom Ethics*, 336.

3

Kudzu

Thy kingdom come, thy will be done
on earth as it is in heaven.

WITH THE THIRD SET of clauses, "Thy kingdom come, thy will be done on earth as it is in heaven," we not only enter the heart of the prayer, but we approach the very heart of Jesus's message and mission.

In the first chapter of the first gospel to be written, Mark gives a succinct summary of Jesus's message: "Now after John was arrested, Jesus came to Galilee, proclaiming the good news of God, and saying, 'The time is fulfilled, and the kingdom of God has come near; repent and believe in the good news'" (Mark 1:14–15). Jesus's essential message was about the "kingdom of God." But what did he mean by that phrase? And how does God's kingdom relate to the various kingdoms of the world? Do they overlap? Do they coexist or cooperate, or are they in irreconcilable conflict?

I will explore these questions in this chapter, along with the notion that it is important not only *that* we say these words, but also *how* we say them. This part of the Prayer comes alive when we begin, as the old joke goes, to put the em*pha*sis on the right syl*lab*le.

A KINGDOM NOT IN THE CLOUDS

First, a word about the nature of the kingdom, or reign, of God. In the first chapter, I wrote at some length about the distinction between what the Evangelists meant by those synonymous phrases, "kingdom of God" (Mark and Luke), and "kingdom of heaven" (Matthew) and how popular Christianity has come to misinterpret them and invest them with meanings they were never meant to bear. Even when one calls it the kingdom of *heaven*, the kingdom exists very much in this world, not somewhere in the clouds—in the sweet (and irrelevant) by-and-by.

Does this mean that I do not believe in life after death—in eternal rewards for the faithful and eternal punishments for the wicked? Does it mean I don't "believe . . . in the resurrection of the body and the life everlasting," as the Apostle's Creed puts it?[1]

No, it does not. Well, I do take issue with the *eternal* punishment part, but on the resurrection and some form of life after death I hold fairly orthodox views. Unfortunately, popular Christianity has itself left the realm of orthodoxy and adopted instead a syncretistic mish-mash of biblical, neo-Platonic, and cultural notions about heaven and hell. At least where heaven is concerned, this has resulted in a sentimental and fairly fantastical vision of eternity that at most points comes closer to ridiculous than sublime.

More to the point, and far more harmful to the purposes of God and the continuing work of Jesus, these notions distract our attention from where God wants it to be directed. When we equate the *kingdom of heaven* with *heaven*, we run the risk of devaluing life in this world in favor of life in the next. I have heard people say in all sincerity that this life serves as nothing more than a training ground or trial run, and our only really important task is to make the right decision that will lead us to the proper destination in eternity. That decision may consist in believing in Jesus as Lord and Savior, or submitting wholly to God as an obedient Muslim, or living a life of ethical righteousness, or something else. Whatever the decision may be, if its only purpose is to assure us of some kind of otherworldly reward, it signifies a tunnel-vision approach to life that completely misses the mark when it comes to honoring God and keeping God's name hallowed.

God takes the world and its inhabitants very seriously—God created them, after all—and so should we. God takes life in this world very seriously—the Incarnation provides ample evidence of this truth—and so

---

1. Apostle's Creed, lines 14, 18–19.

should we. So *must* we. One of the purposes of the Lord's Prayer is to adjust our vision so that we begin to see the world from God's perspective. When we pray, "Thy kingdom come, thy will be done on earth as it is in heaven," we are asking God to bring the kingdom in its fullness. Here. Now. And we are telling God that we are on board with this project—that we too want to see God's kingdom come and God's will be done. Here. Now.

The kingdom, or reign, of God, or of heaven—however we may put it—is about justice and equity and redemption and dignity and abundance and community and healing, not in some other world, but in this one. This kingdom stands not in the clouds, but in the soil, the gravel, the flesh and blood of *this* time, *this* place. God desires to bring the kingdom to fruition not after death but during life. Here. Now. When we pray the Prayer, we are committing ourselves—our minds, hearts, blood, sweat, tears, and bank accounts—to the same goal.

THY, NOT THEIRS

"Thy kingdom come, thy will be done" is at once a profound affirmation of our confidence in God and God's purposes and a profound negation. It reminds us that many pitfalls lie in wait on the path of discipleship.

We begin to see this clearly when we make a very simple change in the way we voice this part of the Prayer. Try this experiment: listen to yourself as you say aloud this section of the Prayer the way you ordinarily do in worship (or the way you might if you were to participate in a Christian worship service). "Thy kingdom come, thy will be done on earth as it is in heaven." Where did the emphasis fall? I have recited this prayer in many different churches in wide and varied settings, and the congregations' emphasis almost always falls on the two verbs, "earth," and "heaven." Thy kingdom *come*, thy will be *done* on *earth* as it is in *heaven*."

I can think of a couple of different reasons for this. First, when praying or speaking in unison, a congregation needs to find a certain rhythm to help them stay together. Second, long acquaintance with literary influences ranging from William Shakespeare to Mother Goose has taught us to read poetry, or anything resembling poetry, in iambic pentameter: duh-*dum* duh-*dum* duh-*dum* duh-*dum* duh-*dum*. More precisely, then, our reading of the Prayer goes, "Thy *king*dom *come*, thy *will* be *done* on *earth* as it *is* in *heaven*," with the strongest emphasis falling on *come, done, earth,* and *heaven,* and somewhat less stress—a secondary accent, if you will—on *king,* *will,* and *is.*

Now do this: say the lines again, this time deliberately putting the emphasis on the word "thy." *Thy* kingdom come, *thy* will be done on earth as it is in heaven." Did you hear what just happened? With that simple change, a fresh and intriguing breeze just blew through a prayer that may have become stale through repetition. Instead of the soporific effect of iambic pentameter, a poetic rhythm tailor-made for mindless, rote recitation, we suddenly have a surprising new way of speaking—and hearing—the Prayer.

Consider what happens when you hear someone put the stress of a sentence in an unusual place or somewhere you didn't expect. Your ears perk up, don't they? You may have heard the words countless times before, but this new take on them causes you to listen more closely to try to understand the reason for the change. As a boy, when I heard my mom call out from the other room, "Robert *Scott* Turner," I knew automatically that something was up, and that it was in my best interest to pay attention. Why did she say my name that way? What did I do this time? In the same way, when we hear someone stressing the "thys" in the Prayer, it makes us sit up and take notice. Why did he say it that way? What conclusion are we supposed to draw?

One reasonable conclusion is that the one praying wants to differentiate between God and some unknown other. *Thy* kingdom come—not someone else's kingdom. *Thy* will be done—not someone else's will.

This leads to an obvious follow-up question: who is the someone else? Or we could say, who is the anyone else? If we want *God's* kingdom to come and will to be done, it must mean that we reject not just *someone* else's kingdom and will, but *anyone* and *everyone* else's. *Thy,* not theirs. *Thy,* not mine. *Thy,* not anybody else's but *thine.*

But even with this blanket negation of all other kingdoms, particular kingdoms seem to rise up to clash with God's kingdom at particular points in history. Jesus clearly was making a theological statement—a preference for God's kingdom and will over that of Satan or Beelzebub or any rival pagan gods. But he was also quite explicitly doing something his followers, through long practice, have learned to reject just as explicitly. Jesus was making a pointed statement about his and his followers' political allegiance.

That's right, I said it. Political. Jesus was making a *political* statement. In a prayer, no less. What's more, hundreds of millions of people make the same political statement in church every week, often without even knowing it. Some of those people would rather chew their legs off than mix politics and religion. Yet every Sunday they repeat some of the most radical political rhetoric ever uttered. Because every time we say the words, "Thy kingdom come, thy will be done on earth as it is in heaven," whether we like it or not, we get political.

POLITICAL, POLITICAL, I WANNA GET POLITICAL

Jesus was a political figure. By this I don't mean he was political the way our culture commonly defines the term. In our day the realm of politics has been narrowed in the public mind, in the United States, at least, to refer to not much more than the machinations and intrigues of the two major political parties. Dueling press conferences between the Speaker of the House and the Senate Majority Leader, each trying to put the appropriate spin on the latest squabble. The executive and legislative branches at odds with one another, each seeking to lay the blame or take the credit, as the case may be. And a perpetual campaign cycle, wherein the news media begin speculating about possible candidates in the next general election before the concession speech in the current one. This is largely what "political" has come to mean in our day and age.

Sometimes we use the word in a broader sense, but one closely related to this kind of partisanship. In this case, "political" has come to be practically synonymous with "ideological." In the hyper-polarized, litmus test-crazy culture of twenty-first-century America, to pigeonhole and either embrace or reject another person one need only listen for a few key code words. Choice. Activist judges. Progressive. Limited government. Tax and spend. Law and order. And so on. Sprinkle a few of these in your conversations, tweets, or Facebook posts, and see how quickly you get assigned all the other baggage that comes with the label of conservative or liberal.

Jesus was political in an entirely different way. The word "political" comes from the same root as the Greek word polis, which we usually translate as "city" or "city-state." Beyond the family and clan, the polis was the basic unit of social organization in Ancient Greece. Think Athens and Sparta, for example. "Politics," then, means something along the lines of, "The structuring and functioning of the polis to bring about the greatest benefit for the greatest number of citizens." In Harold Lasswell's classic definition, politics concerns the allocation of resources—who gets what, when, and how.[2] Politics has to do with social relationships: power, equity, protection of the vulnerable, and the balance between individual liberty and community responsibility. It has to do with how people live together so that nobody has too much or too little and each person's intrinsic worth is recognized and respected.

That is the sense in which Jesus was a political figure. He concerned himself with social relationships as much as or more than individual souls. Read the gospels in a language that, like the original Koine Greek and unlike modern English, clearly distinguishes between the second person singular and second person plural pronouns, and count how many times in his teaching Jesus uses the plural "you" versus the singular. Contrary to what many of us who were raised on pietistic Christianity have been taught, Jesus had no interest in saving individual souls so they could detach themselves from the world and live in some hermetically sealed spiritual realm. Rather, he sought to create a community in which the ideals and spirit of the old covenant would be lived out in *this* world. In the words of Oscar Romero, "The Christian faith does not cut us off from the world but immerses us in it; the church is not a fortress set apart from the city. The church follows Jesus, who lived, worked, struggled, and died in the midst of a city, in the polis."[3] Jesus promoted not escapism but radical engagement.

Of course, when you become radically engaged with the world, when you invest yourself in building community and looking to the equitable distribution of resources—in short, when you get political—you will undoubtedly run into resistance from the powers that be. When the have-nots start to get organized, the haves get nervous. And when the haves get nervous, they begin to take measures to put the have-nots back in their place, using intimidation, threats, destruction of property, and outright violence. In Latin America in the late twentieth century the powers' tactics of intimidation and control resulted in thousands of *desaparecidos*—the disappeared—people who had vanished under suspicious circumstances. More often than not, the desaparecidos had been involved in some political activity or had made a disparaging comment about *el presidente* at an inopportune moment. Everyone knew their disappearances were no coincidence, but had resulted from orders by someone in the ranks of the government or military. They were abducted, often tortured, usually killed,

2. See Lasswell, *Politics*.

3. Dennis et al., eds., *Oscar Romero*, 16.

and their bodies dumped in the countryside or in a landfill for their grieving and outraged (but effectively cowed) families to find . . . or not.

Sometimes the intimidation tactics were more subtle, hiding behind the veneer of law and civility. Take the Jim Crow laws that appeared in the American South after Reconstruction and held sway for more than eighty years. The Fifteenth Amendment to the US Constitution gave black people the right to vote, but did nothing to prevent states from instituting poll taxes, literacy tests, and grandfather clauses to effectively keep the voting booths lily white. With the backing of the Supreme Court, states could and did segregate all public facilities. The landmark case *Plessy v. Ferguson* (1896) declared "separate but equal" accommodations constitutional. Without close supervision from outside, however, segregationist governments rigidly enforced the "separate" part while roundly ignoring the "equal" part. Anyone who dared protest against this system risked losing his job, having her house burned or bombed, or being lynched. These methods effectively kept everyone in his or her culturally assigned place.

In Jesus's day, the elites amassed wealth for themselves while keeping their victims from rising up against them. The most important and valued commodity in the agrarian societies of the ancient world was land. Owning even a little bit of land gave one a degree of freedom and autonomy, and at least a chance at prosperity. Owning a lot of land offered the surest way to gain wealth, prestige, and power. So the aristocratic few in first-century Palestine worked out ways to take the land from the impoverished many, allowing the rich to live in even greater luxury while sinking the peasantry into even greater poverty.

Their preferred method for taking land was through the mechanism of debt. We will examine how they went about this in more detail in Chapter 5, but for now suffice it to say that the wealthy landowners had figured out how to manipulate debt to push small freeholders off their land. This cleared the way for them to amass greater and greater holdings, which equated to greater and greater wealth and prestige. Recent excavations in the upper city of Jerusalem reveal that the aristocrats and priests lived in extravagant luxury—the palatial mansion of the high priest Caiaphas near the precincts of the Temple is stunning, one might even say obscene, in its lavishness. This gaudy display of wealth became possible in large part through the priests' land holdings in other parts of Judea, which they had very likely taken from peasants through manipulation of debt. In Galilee, Herod Antipas and his cronies operated the same way. They systematically took over the land until for all practical purposes they held an agribusiness monopoly, the profits from which paid for Herod's showy building projects in Sepphoris and Tiberias and subsidized their own conspicuous consumption.

These were the real-life absentee landowners who for the most part do *not* appear in Jesus's parables but whose shadows loom large in them. Jesus knew about the corruption in the system. He knew about debt slavery, foreclosure, and deceitful, greedy stewards. His family may have been victims of these abuses themselves. Multiply this scenario by the hundreds or thousands throughout Galilee, Judea, and the surrounding region, and you can see the crisis Jesus encountered in the third decade of the first century. You can understand why he took action to redress the situation—why he decided to get political.

WHO SITS ON THE THRONE?

The Torah asserts again and again that God is the true king of Israel. That is why, alongside and interwoven with the Old Testament stories celebrating David and his dynasty, there runs a counter-narrative, a tradition of opposition to the monarchy. If God is the king, to institute a human king is a disobedient act. The counter-tradition depicts as disobedience the Israelites' crowning Saul king to replace the aging judge Samuel. God tells Samuel, "They have not rejected you, but they have rejected me from being king over them" (1 Sam 8:7). God then instructs Samuel to give them their king, but only after warning them in great detail how the king and his descendants will abuse their power and make the people into subjects and slaves rather than free citizens.

Samuel warns them, among other things, that the king will take their land: "He will take the best of your fields and vineyards and olive orchards and give them to his courtiers" (1 Sam 8:14). This is an especially egregious violation, because the Bible says repeatedly that the land belongs to God alone. The people are merely tenants, and should therefore not conceive of their relationship to the land in terms of absolute ownership. God parcels out the land as God sees fit, and no human being has the right to change that, not even a king. Land that starts out in your family stays in your family. Even if you fall on hard times and have to sell your land, the Torah contains a provision that in the fiftieth year, the year of jubilee, all land reverts to its original holder. No one is to be permanently deprived of the sacred legacy of the land.

God is the king. God owns the land. God says who gets it.

One imagines that Jesus must have objected to the tactics the large landowners used to add to their own holdings by taking their poorer neighbors' land. Not only did they steal from their fellow citizens, but they also in a very real sense stole from God. Because God identifies so strongly with the poor, the former offended God just as much as the latter.

In Deuteronomy 15, God declares that, if the people of Israel obey the commandments and remain steadfast in their adherence to the covenant, "there will . . . be no one in need among you, because the LORD is sure to bless you in the land that the LORD your God is giving you as a possession to occupy" (Deut 15:4). We can easily judge how well they did on this score by considering the many instances in which the Bible depicts God's outrage when the rich and powerful act to ensure that needy people do indeed persist in the land, and at the ways they abuse and prey upon them. When Jezebel conspires to have Naboth killed so Ahab can take possession of Naboth's vineyard (see 1 Kgs 21), the prophet Elijah condemns both Jezebel and Ahab in the strongest terms. The prophet Amos voices God's indignation that the wealthy members of Israelite society "[buy] the poor for silver / and the needy for a pair of sandals" (Amos 8:4), and condemns their hypocritical piety:

> I hate, I despise your festivals,
>   and I take no delight in your solemn assemblies.
> Even though you offer me your burnt-offerings and grain-offerings,
>   I will not accept them;
> and the offerings of well-being of your fatted animals
>   I will not look upon.
> Take away from me the noise of your songs;
>   I will not listen to the melody of your harps.
> But let justice roll down like waters,
>   and righteousness like an ever-flowing stream (Amos 5:21–24).

But the words of Isaiah match most closely what the wealthy landowners were doing to the Galilean and Judean peasants of Jesus's day:

> Ah, you who join house to house,
>   who add field to field,
>   until there is room for no one but you,
>   and you are left to live alone

in the midst of the land!" (Isa 5:8).

The aristocratic elites fulfilled this saying precisely through their strategy of annexation by debt and foreclosure. They abused their neighbors, amassed spectacular wealth, and added to the ranks of the landless and discontented peasants struggling each day to keep themselves and their families alive. Worst of all, they acted in direct disobedience to God.

All of this was made possible because of a corrupt Temple hierarchy in Judea and a corrupt tetrarchy in Galilee, both of which enjoyed the backing of Roman law and, more pointedly, Roman military might. Rome sought collaborators among the elites of their subject peoples, who would administer the collection of tribute. In return, they provided protection against the wrath of their dispossessed countryfolk. Basking in the security afforded them by their imperial patrons, the elites, many of whom were members of the priestly caste, built luxurious villas and lived in comfort and safety in the cities, far from those they had victimized.

When Jesus pronounces, "*Thy* kingdom come . . . on earth as it is in heaven," he raises a pointed and potentially very dangerous question: "Who sits on the throne?" Not simply, "Who sits on the throne of your heart?" as I have heard so often in Baptist churches over the years, but who sits on the throne of the world? To whom do you owe your ultimate allegiance? When the chips are down, who do you think is really in charge, and whose side are you (or will you be) on?

Even better than, "Who sits on the throne?" we might ask, "Which throne is most important to you?" In Jesus's time, after all, the Roman Emperor clearly sat on the throne of the world. No one doubted that. Tiberius Caesar ruled an empire that encompassed the Mediterranean basin, reached east into the Arabian peninsula, and stretched north all the way to the English Channel. He held the power of life and death over millions of people, and he had legions ready to enforce that power at a moment's notice.

I hesitate to ask the question this way, however, because of the way many in the church have misunderstood Martin Luther's doctrine of the "two realms." Luther made a clear distinction between spiritual and temporal authority, and said that these two distinct realms should not be confused or intermingled. He understood both realms to have been established by God for the right ordering of life in the world and to submit ultimately to God's authority. Unfortunately, many of Luther's later interpreters lost the nuances of his view. They produced a diluted version of it that has resulted in the over-spiritualization of the religious aspects of life and the over-secularization of the worldly ones. In this popular version of the two realms doctrine, life divides into two discrete spheres—the sacred and the secular—and never the twain shall meet. God has a kingdom, for certain, but it is separate and distinct from the kingdoms of the world.

In our present discussion, these "kingdoms of the world" comprised the kingdom of Caesar over the Roman Empire, the kingdom of Herod Antipas over Galilee, and the quasi-kingdom of the Temple state over all the Jewish residents of Palestine and beyond. The two realms theory would say that these earthly kingdoms properly ruled the secular affairs of politics, economics, and the organization of society, while God was relegated to a kingdom governing the religious realm and the inner lives of individuals. God holds no legitimate place in the world of external relations and the affairs of state. Again, that scene from *Romero* comes to mind:

> Representative of the religious realm: "The gospel has political implications."
> Representative of state power: "We'll take care of those."

Unfortunately, this way of organizing reality ignores the inseparability of sacred and secular, religion and politics, "church" and "state" in premodern societies. An ancient would have found our modern concept of the "wall of separation" between church and state unfathomable. The king represented the gods, and the gods acted as the patrons and protectors of the state. In fact, a religious and patriotic pagan subject of the Empire would have offered sacrifices to, among others, Roma, a goddess who personified the Roman state. Religion and politics were two sides of the same coin. One couldn't separate them even if one had conceived the preposterous notion of trying.

And Jesus wasn't trying. He knew it would be both futile and wrong to attempt to dissect the religious and secular realms. He knew that life is of a piece. But he also knew of more than one claimant to the loyalty of that one indivisible life, and of the impossibility of serving them all. "No one can serve two masters," he said in the Sermon on the Mount, "for a slave will either hate the one and love the other, or be devoted to the one and despise the other" (Matt 6:24). While there may have been two thrones, Caesar's and God's, Jesus knew that one must choose between them. *Thy* kingdom come (not Caesar's). *Thy* will be done (not Herod's). On *earth* (here in the real world of politics, economics, and social relationships) as it is in heaven (where our Father aren't).

Commenting on this part of the Prayer, John Dominic Crossan says, "Heaven is in great shape—earth is where the problems are."[4] Our Father aren't in heaven, because we need God much more desperately down here.

UNDOMESTICATING GOD'S WILL

In addition to the coming of God's kingdom, the Prayer also has us ask that God's will be done. Here we have a good New Testament example of a very common feature in the Old Testament: poetic parallelism. Instead of rhyme or alliteration, which are common in poetry written in English, the ancient Hebrews preferred the poetic device of parallelism. The first line of a couplet makes a statement or employs an image, then the second line restates the content of the first line in different but parallel language. The Psalms, Proverbs, and the prophetic books are loaded with this poetic feature. Take for instance, Psalm 18. Notice how the second line of each of these verses restates or expands upon the first:

> The cords of death encompassed me;
>   the torrents of perdition assailed me;
> the cords of Sheol entangled me;
>   the snares of death confronted me.
> In my distress I called upon the Lord;
>   to my God I cried for help.
> From his temple he heard my voice,
>   and my cry to him reached his ears" (Ps 18:4–6).

We see much the same thing happening in this part of the Lord's Prayer. Jesus says, "Thy kingdom come," then restates the idea in different language, "Thy will be done," in a way that sheds more light on both lines. The second statement simultaneously confirms the first statement and differs from it, and the proximity of the two lines enriches the meanings of both. It's a lot like the oft-quoted verse (I quoted it above, in fact) from the prophet Amos: "Let justice roll down like waters, / and righteousness like an ever-flowing stream" (Amos 5:24). Righteousness and justice, although intimately related, are not exactly the same thing, and the image in the second line of the couplet of a wadi whose waters do not fail during the dry season resembles and yet differs from the image of a waterfall in the first line.

---

4. Crossan, *The Greatest Prayer*, 115.

God's will likewise differs from God's kingdom, although they are closely, even inseparably, related. We could understand the petition for the kingdom to come without the petition about God's will, but the latter reinforces the former and enriches it, and vice versa. It is God's will . . . desire . . . *passion* to bring God's kingdom to fruition in this world. Tying the two ideas together forces us to recognize that the kingdom of God does not sit on God's back burner as some peripheral or ancillary idea, nor does it lie buried on a long list of "to-do" items. Rather, it inhabits the absolute center of who God is and what God is about. You want to know God's will? Look to God's kingdom.

We need to acknowledge this because we have a tendency to domesticate God's will in the same way we try to privatize our faith and spiritualize the kingdom. Jesus's wording here jolts us awake and says, "Don't do that! God's will and the life of discipleship mean more than simply a 'personal relationship' with me. Much more. So pay attention!"

I spent six years as a campus minister in the 1990s, in my first professional position after seminary. To this day I look back on that time as a seminal period in my life. I loved my work with college students; some of my most rewarding experiences in ministry happened while I was their leader; and I find the greatest sense of gratification when I see persons I mentored during their college years doing great things for the kingdom of God.

I mention this because in my work with these students I frequently heard the question, "What is God's will for my life?" The young adult years are a crucial time in a person's emotional, social, and spiritual development, and students feel a lot of pressure to make decisions about career, marriage, and other issues of tremendous importance for their futures. Naturally, they often feel some fear and trembling when faced with these choices. And many conscientious Christian students naturally want some assurance that they are making the right decisions.

Many Christians, especially those of us who were formed in the evangelical tradition, have been trained to understand God's will in intimately personal terms. A lot of us have also come to believe that God has one will for our lives, and if we get it wrong, dire consequences will follow. It therefore becomes crucial to approach important decisions—career, relationships, and so on—with the greatest of care, even trepidation. The pressure is so high, and the person's desire to get it right is so strong, that she may worry herself into immobility. With so many possible paths to follow, and presumably only one correct choice, the safest course may be to stand still and make no choice at all. The students who would come to me with that awful question, "What is God's will?" would very often ask it in an agonized, almost desperate tone of voice. "Help me," was the underlying plea. "I don't want to get this wrong."

I always felt compassion for these students because I had been there often enough myself, but I also felt peeved at the church for having created and fostered this anxiety to no useful purpose. This (mis)understanding of God's will gives rise to much needless angst, and may in fact cause real harm.

If we conceptualize the will of God in purely personal terms, we have failed to grasp the very essence of that will. When we divorce the will of God from the kingdom of God, with all its social and political ramifications, God's will gets domesticated, privatized, *tamed*. The powers that array themselves against God's purposes are quite content to let the discussion of the will of God revolve around the inner life of solitary individuals. Those powers only begin to get nervous when we make the ties between God's will and kingdom explicit, and when we take seriously the part of the Lord's Prayer that looks for God's will to be done *on earth*. Here. Now.

I would tell my students who had fretted themselves to distraction over this question that they already knew God's will. They would then look at me quizzically (or irately, depending on just how wound up they had become), and I would explain that the Bible is chock-full of specific examples of God's will. "What does the Lord require of you but to do justice, and to love kindness, and to walk humbly with your God?" (Mic 6:8). "Love the LORD your God with all your heart, and with all your soul, and with all your might" (Deut 6:5/Mark 12:30).[5] "Love your neighbor as yourself" (Lev 19:18/Mark 12:31). Too easy? Try this one: "Love your enemies and pray for those who persecute you" (Matt 5:44). Or how about this one, which makes it about as explicit as it can get: "Rejoice always, pray continually, give thanks in all circumstances; for *this is God's will for you* in Christ Jesus" (1 Thess 5:16–18 TNIV, emphasis added). If you haven't managed to get all those manifestations of God's will right yet, you shouldn't spend too much mental and spiritual energy on secondary questions.

---

5. Mark's version adds "and with all your mind." Luke and Matthew follow him in this, although Matthew eliminates "and with all your strength." See Matt. 22:37 and Luke 10:27.

By this point, the student in question would have got where I was going. He would say, "I understand all that, but I'm talking about God's specific will for *me*. I still have to declare a major, after all." My response to that would often come across as unsatisfactory to the student, but I still firmly believe it to be true. I would say that if we were to focus our attention and energy on those things that the Scriptures reveal to be clear manifestations of God's will, the other stuff would fall into place. As Jesus puts it in Matthew 6:33, "Strive first for the kingdom of God and [God's] righteousness [or justice], and all these things [food, shelter, clothing, vocation, fulfilling relationships] will be given to you as well."

When you combine this advice with Frederick Buechner's wisdom on the subject of vocation, you can get a pretty reliable read on what God wants you to do. Buechner writes, "The kind of work God usually calls you to is the kind of work (a) that you need most to do and (b) that the world most needs to have done. . . . The place God calls you to is the place where your deep gladness and the world's deep hunger meet."[6]

God's will is not, as surprising as it may seem to some, all about us. It is *partly* about us, but primarily it is about God's vision for the world God loves. Amazingly, God invites us to participate in the effort to bring that vision to reality. For God to guide us to the place where our passions can help soothe the world's deep hunger I find far more compelling and fulfilling than if God were to micromanage our relationships, career choices, and so on. Let God's will be untamed, seek God's kingdom above all else, and let all our other decisions be formed and molded accordingly.

DOMINATION AND ITS DISCONTENTS

The kingdom and will of God are wild and untamed, and can even be dangerous. They especially endanger the "powers and authorities" (to use New Testament terminology) that have a vested interest in the status quo—all the competing kingdoms and wills that lose out when we pray, "*Thy* kingdom come, *thy* will be done." But the kingdom and will of God can endanger even those of us who pray that prayer. We have our own wills, after all, and our own petty kingdoms that we would like nothing better than to establish and expand. God's will and kingdom often conflict with ours, and we can find it difficult and painful to surrender our dreams and desires in favor of God's. We resemble Frodo Baggins standing on the lip of the Cracks of

6. Buechner, *Wishful Thinking*, 118–19.

Doom, mere inches away from completing the quest that has already cost him so much, saying, "I have come . . . but I do not choose now to do what I came to do," and putting on the Ring.[7] Even knowing better than anyone else the awful burden of the Ring, and the terrible consequences of failing in his quest to destroy it, he finds it impossible to surrender his own dreams of lordship. Only through more pain and the loss of a part of himself (both figuratively and literally) can he finally subordinate his will to the will of the wise and good of Middle-Earth who have staunchly defied the Dark Lord Sauron for so long.

In the same way, our surrender to God's will can bring us pain and loss. Jesus knew that the surrender of his will would cost him dearly—his agony in Gethsemane bears eloquent witness to that. Countless others throughout Christian history have suffered similar fates. Peter and Paul. Perpetua and Felicity. Thomas à Becket and Thomas More. Oscar Romero and the four Maryknoll nuns raped and killed in El Salvador only nine months after Romero's own martyrdom. And the nameless multitudes who have borne faithful witness even in the face of ostracism, imprisonment, and death—those whom history has forgotten but God tenderly remembers. All of these "learned obedience through what [they] suffered" (Heb 5:8) and came to know just how dangerous God's will and kingdom can be.

And for what? To all appearances, the sacrifices of saints, martyrs, and heroes of the faith have not brought the fullness of the kingdom. The world looks just as dark as it ever has, and the powers seem just as firmly entrenched and in control as ever. We've been praying for God's kingdom to come and will to be done for nearly two millennia now, and what do we have to show for it?

Not an awful lot, perhaps. But then again, maybe more than we imagine. When thinking about the kingdom of God, we need to bear in mind that God specializes in small things. God has gone about God's business in a curious way throughout salvation history, frequently choosing those the world considers small and insignificant to accomplish remarkable things. Consider the following examples from the biblical record:

- God consistently forgoes the firstborn in favor of younger children. God chooses Jacob over Esau, Ephraim over Manasseh, David over his seven older brothers, and so on.

7. Tolkien, *The Lord of the Rings*, 945.

- God works with the least likely of characters to carry out God's great purposes. Jacob is a liar and swindler; Moses is a murderer with a speech impediment; Sarah becomes a nursing mother as a nonagenarian; Ruth is a pagan foreigner who becomes the grandmother of Israel's greatest king; Peter is an uneducated fisherman; Paul is one who had persecuted the church.

- God brings about amazing results from seemingly insignificant beginnings. Gideon defeats the Midianite army with a force of only three hundred men armed with torches, trumpets, and pottery; the Israelites go down to Egypt as a band of seventy people and emerge as a great multitude; and the *pièce de résistance*: a child wrapped in rags and laid in a cattle trough—after being born to parents so poor they can't even afford the regular sacrifice for redeeming a firstborn son—grows up to become the Savior of the World.

God does indeed specialize in small things.

Jesus confirms this in many of his parables. A farmer scatters seed rather haphazardly, with only a few grains landing on arable soil, but those seeds sprout and produce a mega-bumper crop: a hundredfold harvest. A woman takes a tiny pinch of yeast and kneads it into her dough, and that pinch leavens the entire batch. A mustard seed, the smallest of all seeds, grows into a tree where birds can build their nests.

In the parable of the mustard seed we encounter one of the more puzzling enigmas in Jesus's repertoire of stories and one-liners. For one thing, Jesus is either using poetic license or he flunked botany, because the mustard seed is demonstrably *not* the smallest of all seeds, and it grows into a shrub or bush that only with a generous imagination could be described as a tree.[8] But aside from these technicalities, this analogy poses a much more confusing, even troubling problem: the mustard plant is an invasive weed that no farmer would wish to grow within a mile of her fields.[9] It is

---

8. Joachim Jeremias suggests that Jesus may be alluding to a metaphor the prophet Ezekiel uses for the faithful remnant of Israel. In Ezek. 17:22–24, God promises to plant a sprig from a cedar tree on a high mountain, and care for it so that it will flourish. "Under it," Ezekiel writes in v. 23, "every kind of bird will live; in the shade of its branches will nest winged creatures of every kind." See Jeremias, *Rediscovering the Parables*, 118.

9. John Dominic Crossan writes, "That, said Jesus, was what the Kingdom was like: not like the mighty cedar of Lebanon and not quite like a common weed, [but] like a pungent shrub with dangerous takeover properties. Something you would want in only small and carefully controlled doses—if you could control it." See Crossan, *The Historical Jesus*, 279.

an objectionable, troublesome species of plant life. And Jesus chooses it to describe the kingdom of God! What was he thinking?

In our context, it would be like comparing the kingdom of God to the northern snakehead, a species of fish native to Africa and Asia that has begun to appear in waterways in the United States, most notably in the Potomac River in Virginia and Maryland. Snakeheads have no natural predators in these new areas, and they reproduce so rapidly that they now threaten to eradicate a number of native species and upset the balance of entire ecosystems. It would be like comparing the advance of God's reign and the accomplishment of God's purposes to the advance of the invasive kudzu vine across the landscape of the American South.

These are surprising images, to say the least, but surprise was precisely what Jesus had in mind. The growth of God's kingdom is a surprise whenever it happens. It can increase rapidly from small, unpromising beginnings. And it serves as a source of vexation to the powers that control the world system. In short, the kingdom of God is a nuisance.

A word about the idea that powers other than God control the world is in order. Christian theology, and pretty much any creed or confession of faith you want to consider, holds as a given that God is sovereign over the world God created. But that's not the "world" in question here. Paul had a special use for the word "world" (*kosmos*). He used it to describe the fallen world—the web of culture, philosophy, power relationships, and human systems—that, as a result of the Fall, opposes or rebels against the purposes of God. Self-centeredness, greed, xenophobia, fear, and violence characterize the kosmos. Walter Wink has given the name "the Domination System" to this "world."[10] Brian McLaren writes of "the suicide machine."[11] John Dominic Crossan and Marcus Borg call it "the normalcy of civilization"[12]— simply a description of the way things are.

I prefer Wink's terminology because it clearly shows that, at its heart, the contrast between the world opposed to God and God's vision for the world is a contrast in *power relationships*. To borrow the terminology of feminist theology, the Domination System exercises "power-over"—a hierarchical arrangement in which the strong dominate the weak and might makes right. It is the world of patriarchalism, in which men hold power over women, adults over children, the rich over the poor, the armed over

10. Wink, *Engaging the Powers*, 9.

11. McLaren, *Everything Must Change*, 5.

12. Borg and Crossan, *The Last Week*, 8.

the unarmed, and so on. Competition, not cooperation, serves as the *modus operandi* in this zero-sum game. In a system defined by "power-over," there has to be someone on top and someone else on bottom. The latter seeks to get out from under the thumb of those on top and reverse the positions. That's why revolutions almost never bring fundamental change. The oppressed revolutionaries quickly become oppressors themselves when they take over the top spot. As long as both groups play by the same rules, the sick, violent, wasteful game will go on. Bruce Springsteen hits the nail on the head, as he so often does, in this line from "Atlantic City": "Down here it's just winners and losers / and don't get caught on the wrong side of that line."[13]

By contrast, God's power can best be described as "power-with." Instead of competition, cooperation prevails. Instead of hierarchical, top-down power relationships, people share power. Instead of an economy of fear that drives all participants to use violence either to seize power or maintain it, God's world operates on an economy of love and community. Instead of "it's just winners and losers," the governing sentiment is "we're all in this together."

The quintessential expression of the Domination System's power-over mentality in the first century was, of course, the Roman Empire. Rome used violence and conquest to gain control, and violence and intimidation to maintain it. The celebrated *Pax Romana*, or Roman Peace, was made possible and backed up by the ever-present threat of brutal, violent repression personified by the legions.

Jesus, by contrast, came preaching and implementing a new way of doing things that rejected domination and exercised power-with. He said, "Do not call anyone on earth 'father,' for you have one Father, and he is in heaven" (Matt 23:9 TNIV), thereby signaling the demise of patriarchalism in his new society. He defied social conventions by sharing table fellowship with persons at every level of social status. He outraged traditionalists by accepting women as disciples, incorporating collaborationists (Levi the tax-gatherer) and freedom fighters (Simon the Zealot) into the same group, and performing healings and granting forgiveness outside the established channels of the authoritative priesthood and Temple system.

In the most stunning contrast with the Domination System, Jesus rejected the use of force or violence to prevent his own arrest, and forbade his disciples to choose that path either. He went to his death at the hands of the

13. Springsteen, "Atlantic City."

official representatives of the Domination System "like a lamb that is led to the slaughter" (Isa 53:7; see also Acts 8:30–35), and absorbed in his own person all the violence and hate they could dish out without responding in kind. In so doing, he unmasked the powers that ran the Domination System, revealing them for who they were at their core, and decisively broke their "strong" power-over with the "weakness" of his power-with.[14] The writer of the Epistle to the Colossians puts it this way: "Having disarmed the powers and authorities, he made a public spectacle of them, triumphing over them by the cross" (Col 2:15 TNIV).

Twenty centuries later, Mahatma Gandhi would do the same thing on his Salt March, which exposed the brutality that lay beneath the genteel veneer of the British colonial system and paved the way for Indian independence. The same thing happened three decades later, when young protesters bravely and without violent retaliation faced firehoses and police dogs in the streets of Birmingham. In doing so, they stripped bare before the eyes of the entire nation the true violent nature of segregation and its enforcers, such as Birmingham's Commissioner of Public Safety Eugene "Bull" Connor. In his final speech, an address to the supporters of the striking Memphis sanitation workers on the night before his murder, Martin Luther King Jr. described what happened in Birmingham this way:

> We would move out of the 16th Street Baptist Church day after day; by the hundreds we would move out. And Bull Connor would tell them to send the dogs forth, and they did come; but we just went before the dogs singing, "Ain't gonna let nobody turn me around." Bull Connor next would say, "Turn the fire hoses on." [But] Bull Connor didn't know history. He knew a kind of physics that somehow didn't relate to the trans-physics that we knew about. And that was the fact that there was a certain kind of fire that no water could put out. . . .
>
> [W]e just went on before the dogs and we would look at them; and we'd go on before the water hoses and we would look at it, and we'd just go on singing, "Over my head I see freedom in the air." And then we would be thrown in the paddy wagons, and sometimes we were stacked in there like sardines in a can. And they would throw us in, and old Bull would say, "Take 'em off," and they did; and we would just go in the paddy wagon singing, "We Shall Overcome." And every now and then we'd get in jail, and we'd see the jailers looking through the windows being moved by our prayers, and being moved by our words and our songs. And there

14. See Wink, *Engaging the Powers*, 151–2.

was a power there which Bull Connor couldn't adjust to; and so we ended up transforming Bull into a steer, and we won our struggle in Birmingham.[15]

Whether you call it the Domination System, the normalcy of civilization, the suicide machine, or whatever, the Greek word kosmos speaks of a world opposed to God and God's purposes. Jesus tacitly acknowledges the reality of this system, and the control of the kosmos by powers other than God, in two ways. First, both his proclamation that "the kingdom of God has drawn near" (Mark 1:15) and the very petition we are considering, "Thy kingdom come," themselves indicate that the reins of the kosmos rest in other hands than God's. A second acknowledgement comes in the story of Jesus's temptation in the wilderness (Matt 4, Luke 4). The devil leads him up a high mountain, displays to him all the kingdoms and wealth of the earth, and tells him, "I will give you all of this if you bow down and worship me." What happens next is telling. Jesus does not call the devil a liar, or dispute his claim in any way. He simply quotes Deuteronomy 6:13, saying, "Worship the Lord your God, and serve only him."[16] Clearly Jesus accepts the devil's claim to possess enough authority over the kingdoms of the world to be able to give them to whomever he chooses. After all, it wouldn't be much of a temptation if he couldn't back it up.

When Jesus talks about the kingdom coming, he conveys the image of an insurgent force seeking to wrest control of territory from the dominant group. He speaks in terms of stealth. A seed grows in secret. A woman "hides" yeast in a batch of dough, and it does its leavening work quietly. A man finds treasure buried in a field, then re-buries it until he can obtain the resources to buy the field. Jesus also uses imagery that could almost be described as guerrilla tactics: in one parable someone comes at night and sows weeds in an enemy's wheat field in an act of sabotage.

Jesus paints a picture of the kingdom's manifestations as small rebel outposts in enemy territory. The bulk of the world still rests in the hands of the powers, but in patches, God's reign has gained a foothold. With every act of resistance to the Domination System—every time someone acts selflessly or sacrificially for the benefit of others; every instance in which someone meets violence not with counter-violence but with peaceful resistance

---

15. King Jr., "I See the Promised Land," 281–2.

16. This loose quotation appears in Matt. 4:10. The actual verse from Deuteronomy reads, "The Lord your God you shall fear; him you shall serve, and by his name alone you shall swear."

and tough-minded love; every time someone commits the courageous act of speaking an unpopular truth or defending a principle in the face of pressure, intimidation, or ostracism—another foot of ground gets taken from the enemy.

It doesn't seem like much in the grand scheme of things, but remember, God specializes in small things. And like the mustard plant or the snakehead, each of these small things poses a threat to the status quo in which the powers hold sway. That is why the powers work so hard to saturate the world with their way of doing things (power-over) and why they seek to brainwash entire cultures with their myth of redemptive violence. Their fear of these tiny advances by the Resistance explains why the Domination System nurtures greed, self-involvement, and indifference. They do all these things because they know, as Jesus did, that the puny mustard seed is a terrible nuisance that can overwhelm one's garden practically overnight. They know that kudzu, once it gets its tendrils latched onto a tree, a fence, or a barn, won't stop growing and spreading until it has completely swallowed up the obstacle.

The cover of *Murmur*, the first album by R.E.M., a band that hailed from Athens, Georgia, depicts an abandoned railroad structure completely covered in kudzu. The vines have spread over the trees, the field, and the structure itself. One imagines that if the photographer who took that picture went back a few months or years later, she would be hard-pressed even to find the right location again.[17] That's the power that lies in small things. That's the power of the kingdom of God, and the promise of what will happen to the Domination System when the world-devouring wave of God's reign comes crashing in its fullness.

And so we pray, as members of the Resistance, with fervent and defiant hope, "*Thy* kingdom come, *thy* will be done on earth as it is in heaven."

---

17. R.E.M., *Murmur*. The liner notes credit Sandra Lee Phipps with "photography and art design." A YouTube video from 2011 shows the ravine depicted on the album cover remarkably unchanged after nearly three decades, except that the kudzu has taken on the properties of a wall-to-wall carpet: http://www.youtube.com/watch?v=8r-z7VGIXl4.

4

Different Audiences

Give us this day our daily bread . . .

THE NEXT PETITION IN the Lord's Prayer, "Give us this day our daily bread," is one that those of us who are first-world Christians think we understand, but probably don't. To do so, we need to consider liberation theology's notion of *social location*. Our context profoundly affects our understanding of theological ideas and biblical texts (and history, sociology, psychology, and a host of other areas of human experience and thought, for that matter). Geography, age, gender, race, disability status, level of education, sexual orientation, and socio-economic class all come into play and help determine how we interpret and even how we *hear* the biblical story. My particular social location as a white American male with twenty-four years of schooling and a blue-collar background can make me highly sensitive to certain ideas and themes in Scripture, and for all intents and purposes blind and deaf to others.

Let's look at an example from the book of Genesis. Every Sunday School lesson I ever learned about the patriarch Joseph, and the lion's share of the sermons I have heard and books I have read since, portrayed him as a thoroughly heroic figure. Joseph is the paragon of wisdom, forbearance, and grace in the Old Testament. His jealous brothers sell him into slavery. He flees from the wiles of the "wicked woman," who in retaliation falsely accuses him of attempted rape and lands him in prison. A model inmate, he does a big favor for one of his fellow prisoners, an official in the royal court, who upon his release forgets he's ever heard of Joseph and leaves him to cool his heels in jail for two more years. Finally, through a curious train of circumstances, he comes into Pharaoh's court and, because of his wisdom, quickly rises to a position of prominence second only to Pharaoh himself. Through his prudent policies during seven years of abundance, wherein he takes a percentage of every farmer's harvest and stores it in granaries, he preserves enough food to help the people survive the seven years of terrible famine that follow. Through his wisdom and foresight, he becomes the savior not only of Egypt but also of the Hebrew people. He tops it all off by magnanimously extending grace and forgiveness to the brothers who wronged him so heinously years before.[1] If you were looking for a biblical character to emulate, you couldn't do much better than Joseph.

What these lessons and sermons never mentioned, however, and what I never saw on my own until Walter Brueggemann opened my eyes to it through his commentary on Genesis, was how Joseph went about his "salvation" of the people, and what its effects were.[2] Commentators consistently describe Joseph as "wise," and it's hard to argue with that assessment. Another appropriate word, however, might be "shrewd," which offers something less than an unambiguously ringing endorsement. During the years of plenty, Joseph instituted the policy of taking a portion of the Egyptians' grain harvests and placing it in massive storehouses he had built for that purpose. Joseph and Pharaoh undoubtedly considered this legitimate taxation for the public good. The farmers, on the other hand, might well have called it extortion or something worse. When the famine hit and the people came to Joseph, begging for grain, he opened the storehouses . . . for a price. He sold back to the people the grain he had taken from them in the first place. When all the people's money was gone and the famine still raged, Joseph offered to trade them grain for their livestock. When he had all the livestock, he began taking the people's land in exchange for grain. Genesis 47:20–21 offers this summary: "So Joseph bought all the land in Egypt for Pharaoh. The Egyptians, one and all, sold their fields, because the famine was too severe for them. The land became Pharaoh's, and Joseph reduced the people to servitude, from one end of Egypt to the other."

---

1. Apart from a brief interruption in chapter 38, Joseph's entire story can be found in Genesis 37–50.

2. Brueggeman, "Genesis," 356.

This episode paints a much less flattering portrait of Joseph than does the common storyline of his unadulterated purity and wisdom. And it's right there in the Bible—why had I never seen it?

Liberation theology suggests that I hadn't seen it because my social location—the relative privilege I enjoy because of my background, my country of origin, and the pigmentation of my skin—did not permit me to see it. I benefit every day from being a citizen of the United States, a nation that operates on a global scale very similarly to how Joseph operated in Egypt. I benefit from many perks and comforts that come from collaboration with the Domination System (and silent acquiescence does indeed equal collaboration), so it is in my best interest not to read the Joseph story from the perspective of the victims of his "salvation." Because as soon as your eyes are opened and you read it that way, you face an insistent question: "What am I going to do about it?" Or, as Gilead, a peace advocate in East Jerusalem, says about injustice in his homeland, "Once you see, you can never un-see."[3]

As we reflect on the petition for daily bread, let us try to hear it from a different perspective. The Scriptures have different audiences. Let us try to put ourselves in the shoes and the social location of Jesus's original listeners.

PREACHING TO THE POOR

Historical Jesus scholars often disagree about the social location of Jesus himself. While no reputable expert would go so far as to claim Jesus was rich, they do debate the level of affluence Jesus and his family did or did not enjoy. Some point to his designation in the gospels as a carpenter and say that indicates he belonged to an artisan class and therefore had some modest means.

---

3. My friend Ghassan Tarazi tells the story of his encounter with Gilead (last name unknown), a Jew who works for the Israeli Committee Against House Demolitions and takes pilgrims on tours of the Arab section of East Jerusalem to witness the ugly realities of life under the Israeli occupation. On the bus that was taking a group on a tour of Palestinian homes that had been bulldozed by the Israeli authorities, often with less than a day's notice, Gilead said, "I'm not going to say anything; I just want you to look at your surroundings as we go from West Jerusalem to East Jerusalem." After they witnessed the stark contrast in living conditions between the two sections of the city, and recognized that Israeli policies and oppression bore much responsibility for that contrast, he said, "Once you see, you can never un-see." Ghassan reports that it was a powerful experience for everyone in the group, and it renewed his commitment to work for a just peace in Palestine and Israel.

Others argue that the Greek word we translate as "carpenter," *tekton*, did not carry the same connotation of a skilled professional as our word does. Rather, it described an unskilled laborer who ranked considerably lower on the socio-economic food chain than the other scholars' imagined artisan would have. Some even go so far as to suggest that, in a predominately agrarian economy, a landless tekton would have had even less status than we might expect. John Dominic Crossan, for one, asserts that for Jesus, and his father Joseph before him, to be called tektons would have meant that they were peasants who had lost their land and were now reduced to subsistence-level work as common laborers.[4] One or both of them may have performed unskilled labor in Sepphoris, the sparkling city about three miles northwest of Nazareth that Herod Antipas rebuilt after its razing by the Roman legions. Crossan claims that, far from denoting membership in some sort of comfortably situated artisan class, Jesus's designation as a tekton would have brought him no status, and may even have been a badge of dishonor.

For a couple of different reasons, I favor the interpretation that places Jesus farther down the social scale. First, I find any claim that Jesus was relatively well-off suspect. I fear that a trace of self-justification may have crept into the work of first-world interpreters with an unconscious need to make Jesus's social location more compatible with their own. Second, Jesus addresses his stories, parables, and actions—his entire mission, as a matter of fact—to the poorest of the poor. He populates his parables with day-laborers, tenant farmers, stewards, and absentee landowners. He stays away from urban areas until his fateful trip to Jerusalem, and for the most part he confines his mission to the fishing villages and towns along the shores of the Sea of Galilee and the surrounding countryside—places where the poor, displaced, and disaffected, not the wealthy and powerful, live. Finally, according to Luke, Jesus takes as the overarching theme of his ministry the words of Third Isaiah: "The Spirit of the Lord is upon me and he has sent me to proclaim good news *to the poor* . . . " (Luke 4:18, loosely quoting Isa 61:1; emphasis added).

In the last analysis, we don't know Jesus's level of affluence, or lack thereof, with any certainty or precision. But it doesn't really matter. What matters is that, either because he lives among destitute and desperate people and has compassion for their plight, or because he *shares* their plight, Jesus identifies with the poorest of the poor. In the Sermon on the Mount and the

4. Crossan, *The Birth of Christianity*, 349–50.

vast majority of his other teachings and pronouncements we find examples of someone preaching to the poor.

In Matthew, the Lord's Prayer comes in the context of that very Sermon, and Luke's version comes in response to the disciples' request that Jesus teach them to pray, as John the Baptist had taught his own disciples. That is, they want a formal prayer that will distinguish them as disciples of Jesus. So the Lord's Prayer really functions as a model prayer, a sort of template for what kinds of petitions to bring to God and what kind of attitude to bring to prayer. When prayed together in a group setting, it serves as *the* distinctive prayer of the church.

If this is true, it follows that, because Jesus preaches to the poor in the Sermon on the Mount and teaches his (mostly) poor disciples in Luke, the Lord's Prayer is a prayer of and for poor people. Those of us who are *not* poor must continually bear that in mind as we listen in.

EAVESDROPPING BY THE RICH

When it comes to understanding Jesus's teaching in the New Testament gospels, most of us reading this book are, in essence, eavesdroppers. If Jesus taught, preached to, healed, and organized the poor, and if the Lord's Prayer is a prayer of the poor, most of us reading (or writing) this book are almost certainly outsiders. We are the rich.

A characteristic foible of human nature, and strong evidence of our *fallen* nature, is our tendency to compare and contrast ourselves with others in ways that serve our own interests and ego needs. We have manifold reasons for this behavior, including fear, insecurity, envy, guilt, malice, or simple narcissism. Whatever the reason, many of us do this when the question of wealth and privilege arises. Think about your internal reaction when you read the sentence that ended the last paragraph: "We are the rich." Did you experience any kind of automatic, visceral reaction, either in agreement or disagreement? Did that bald assertion make you feel uncomfortable? Angry? Guilty? Proud? Blasé? Many people, when you describe them as rich, hastily respond, "Oh, no, I'm not rich. Our family is comfortable, sure, but we're not rich by any means. Warren Buffett is rich. The Queen of England is rich. Not me."

Notice how quickly we raise the contrasts, and always with *wealthier* people. We don't need a gap as wide as those in my example, either. One doesn't have to compare oneself to Bill Gates or some Kuwaiti sheikh, and in fact it may be more powerful when we consider subtler differences. One only has to compare oneself with the co-worker who lives in a more upscale section of town, or the neighbor whose house and yard are a little bigger and whose cars are always newer and more expensive than one's own. One still benefits from the comparison.

But what benefits do we reap, exactly? If we compare ourselves with persons who are *more* wealthy, doesn't that contradict the notion that we make the comparisons in order to meet our ego needs?

Not at all. The reason for this—and here we get to the crux of the matter—is that we first-worlders, especially those of us who are members of the dominant ethnic and racial group, have some deep-seated guilt feelings about the wealth and privileges we enjoy. In certain contexts they call this White Liberal Guilt. I believe that many, if not most, of us have a gnawing sense, whether conscious or not, that we do not deserve our good fortune, and we suspect it may legitimately cause those who do not share it to resent us. It becomes understandable, then, that we would deny our wealth or try to soften its negative impact by reaching for examples of those whose good fortune is even good-er and possibly even less deserved than our own. In this we resemble children whose mother has caught them scarfing down Oreos before dinner. Both children are clearly guilty of the infraction, but one of them invariably points a finger and says, "He ate more of them than I did!"

If we seriously want to understand what Jesus is saying in the Prayer and elsewhere, and even more so if we have a notion that we want to follow Jesus as his disciples, we are going to have to grow up and acknowledge the plain facts. Namely, that compared to most of the rest of the world, citizens of the US, Canada, and the European Union possess fabulous, disproportionate, some might even say obscene wealth. Even those of us who can point to six different houses on our block where people more well-off than we live. We *are* the rich. Unless we make serious adjustments to our thinking, we will never be capable of anything more than eavesdropping on the poor. For justice to be done, we must make changes. *Sacrifices*, even. If we ever wish to develop an understanding of and solidarity with the poor—of Jesus's day and our own—we must become more than eavesdroppers. We must become empathetic listeners. We must become advocates. We must become co-laborers.

OUR BREAD FOR TOMORROW

Let's take a closer look at the petition about bread: "Give us this day our daily bread." If we can manage to break through the crust (no pun intended) of endless rote recitation and hear this sentence with fresh ears, we may notice something odd about it. Namely, it is redundant. Give us *this day* our *daily* bread. Why not just say, "Give us our daily bread," or, "Give us bread today," or something straightforward like that? What's the point of the repetition?

The redundancy may be explained as a quirk of translation. An uncommon Greek word, *epiousion*, appears in both Matthew's and Luke's versions of the Prayer. Scholars find this word notoriously difficult to translate or even define accurately. Suggested translations for epiousion include "for today," "for the coming day," and "necessary for existence," but the glossary of my Greek New Testament effectively captures the overall scholarly opinion when it notes that the word is "of doubtful meaning."[5]

Amy-Jill Levine has suggested an alternative translation of the petition: "Give us tomorrow's bread today."[6] Another way of putting it would be, "Give us this day our bread for tomorrow." This translation makes perfect sense when we recall who constituted Jesus's primary audience—the ones on whom we are eavesdropping. Many of them were destitute peasants who had fallen victim to the predatory practices of their wealthy neighbors, as we will see in some detail in the next chapter, and had lost their land. Unjust taxation and manipulation of debt had pushed them off land that had been in their families for generations and pushed them to the brink of penury and starvation. The lucky ones were allowed to stay as sharecroppers on their old farms, but many had to turn to the uncertain livelihood of the unskilled laborer scrounging to make a denarius here and there as a carpenter or tanner. Jesus's famous parable of the workers in the vineyard (Matt 20:1–15) depicts well the desperation of day-laborers who wait in the village marketplace for hours on end, hoping for even an hour or two of work in the afternoon so they could maybe buy a handful of millet or barley to feed their families a little bread.

Unlike most of us, these people knew what it meant to be truly hungry. They knew what it felt like not to know where their next meal was going to come from. They knew the anguish of hearing their children whimper because they simply had nothing to feed them. And because there was no

---

5. Newman, *Concise Greek-English Dictionary*, 70.

6. Levine, *The Misunderstood Jew*, 47–48.

social safety net—no Medicaid, no SNAP, no Social Security—many of them knew firsthand the impotent rage and pain of watching loved ones grow weak and die because they couldn't get enough calories to stay alive.

These people understood, not cerebrally, but in a gut-wrenching way, the many conflicting emotions bound up in the petition, "Give us today our bread for tomorrow." For them, there was nothing academic about this part of the Lord's Prayer. It represented the life-or-death cry of those who knew how severely limited their options were and knew they had little choice but to cast themselves on the mercy of their God. Their Father who aren't in heaven.

When we stop eavesdropping and seek to enter into the social location and circumstances of the people Jesus was speaking to, we see again that the Lord's Prayer is not as simple as it at first appears. The Prayer has an edge to it—a sharp edge that will cut us if we handle it carelessly—and we cannot help but feel the keenness of that edge in the petition for bread. The person who prays, "Give us today our bread for tomorrow," makes a bold request—almost a demand. She issues a defiant challenge to God to keep the promise to care for God's children. Later in the Sermon on the Mount, Jesus will assure his listeners that God does care for them and values them highly. He will counsel them not to worry but to trust in the God who wants always to "give good gifts to those who ask [God]" (Matt 7:11). The petition for the "bread for tomorrow" applies that teaching in a bold way, as though one were throwing down a gauntlet before God and saying, "You've made a lot of promises; now put your money where your mouth is."

The request can be considered bold for another reason—one that alludes to a story from the Hebrew Scriptures. God has just delivered the Israelites from slavery in Egypt, and now they find themselves traveling through a barren wilderness. In Exodus 16, the people grumble to Moses because he has led them into this wasteland where they will surely starve to death. They would have been better off, they whine, to have remained in Egypt where at least they had food. Better a slave in Egypt than a skeleton in the desert.

In response to these complaints, Moses tells the people that God will feed them with a mysterious "bread" from heaven, and instructs them on how to appropriate this gracious gift. Every night, a strange white substance will settle with the dew all around the Israelites' camp. The people call the substance *manna*, a word that basically means, "What the heck *is* this stuff? Oh, who cares? It tastes pretty good," or something along those lines. Every morning they are to collect what they need for that day. Larger families would gather more; smaller families would gather less. They can only collect it in the morning, but it stays fresh for the entire day. If, however, they disobey and collect more than they need for the day, with the intention of storing it up for the following day, they invariably find it moldy and worm-ridden the next morning.

The only exception to this rule has to do with the Sabbath. Because God has commanded the Israelites to set aside the seventh day of the week as a day of complete rest on which no one is to do any regular work, God tells them to gather a double portion of manna on the morning of the sixth day. Unlike what happens every other time they try to hoard it, the manna they collect on Friday remains unspoiled and perfectly fresh all throughout Saturday. Those who fail to get the memo, and go out on the morning of the Sabbath, find to their chagrin that the manna store is closed on Saturdays, and their families go hungry until Sunday morning.

The lessons here are obvious, although not necessarily easy to learn and internalize. God wants the people to trust in God alone to provide for them. Reinhold Niebuhr says that one way our fallen nature clearly reveals itself is when the anxiety over our finitude leads us to seek security in ourselves, or in any source other than God.[7] The hoarders have failed to trust God, seeking instead to meet their family's needs through their own resourcefulness. They pay the price with a bread box full of weevils and rotten manna.

The rules about collecting a double portion on the sixth day reinforce God's trustworthiness. When God says so, you can gather enough for two days and trust that it will last. Then, on the first day of the week, everyone starts from scratch again. You come with empty hands, trusting God to fill them with something that will fill your belly as well.

That's what makes this petition so daring. Jesus guides the people to pray for that double portion for the Sabbath—tomorrow's bread today. It is a prayer of faith: the petitioner seeks sustenance from God and no other

---

7. Niebuhr writes (in gender-exclusive language, unfortunately), "In short, man, being both free and bound, both limited and limitless, is anxious. Anxiety is the inevitable concomitant of the paradox of freedom and finiteness in which man is involved. Anxiety is the internal precondition of sin . . . [and] both the source of creativity and a temptation to sin. . . . The ambition of man to be something is always partly prompted by the fear of meaninglessness which threatens him by reason of the contingent character of his existence. His creativity is therefore always corrupted by some effort to overcome contingency by raising precisely what is contingent to absolute and unlimited dimensions. This effort . . . is always destructive" (Niebuhr, *Nature and Destiny*, 182, 185–6).

source. It is a prayer of hope: the one praying hopes for the relative abundance of the double portion. And it is a prayer of challenge: God, keep your promises!

THE SCANDAL OF HUNGER IN GOD'S WORLD

We cannot avoid, however, the uncomfortable fact that not everyone who prays for their bread for tomorrow gets even their bread for today. Hunger rages in many parts of the world. Starvation and diseases related to hunger or the lack of safe drinking water abound. Diseases such as dysentery and cholera, which those of us in the developed world have taken for granted to be relics of the past, still stalk their prey with vigor in the global South. Consider the following snapshots of hunger in the US and around the world:

- 870 million people in the world are hungry.
- 20,864 people die from hunger-related causes every day.
- Nearly 1.5 billion people in the developing world live in extreme poverty, defined as living on less than $1.25 a day.
- In 2008, nearly nine million children died before they reached their fifth birthday—one-third of these deaths were directly or indirectly due to hunger and malnutrition.
- 178 million of the world's children under five are stunted due to malnutrition.
- 14.5 percent of households in the United States struggle to put food on the table—more than one in five children live in these households.
- In the US, more than 90 percent of SNAP benefits (food stamps) are used up by the third week of the month.[8]

These are scandalous statistics. How, we ask ourselves, can this possibly be true in this day and age? Why have we not yet conquered hunger and put chronic malnutrition on the same list as the dodo or the passenger pigeon? In a world of such extraordinary abundance, a world in which every major religious or ethical tradition instructs its adherents to care for the vulnerable and feed the hungry, how can these problems persist? It is a scandal for which we are all answerable.

8. Bread for the World, "About Hunger."

Bruce Cockburn's song, "If I Had a Rocket Launcher," expresses elo-
quently the helplessness and rage persons of conscience feel when they encounter intractable injustice and the suffering caused by unspeakable evil.
He sings:

> On the Rio Lacantún one hundred thousand wait
> to fall down from starvation or some less humane fate.[9]

I know what he is getting at, but I find it hard to imagine anything
more inhumane than the slow, wasting death of starvation, especially when
we consider that, according the UN's World Food Programme and many
other reputable sources, the world produces more than enough food to feed
everyone.[10] What could be more obscene than the contrast between the way
we gorge ourselves here in the "First World," or the number of *tons* of food
we throw away every day, and the agony of parents in the "Third World"
who must watch their children under the age of five die from hunger-related causes at the staggering rate of more than 17,000 *per day*?[11]

I call this a scandal, rather than a tragedy or an unfortunate state
of affairs, because human greed and sin have in large part created these
problems, and because, although we have the power to change things, the
problems persist. That's what enraged Cockburn so much when he traveled
to Guatemala in the early 1980s and witnessed the atrocities that led to
the scenes of starvation on the Rio Lacantún: the avoidability of it and the
culpability of those in power for allowing it to happen. He makes this clear
in another verse:

> Here comes the helicopter—second time today.
> Everybody scatters and hopes it goes away.
> How many kids they've murdered only God can say.
> If I had a rocket launcher, I'd make somebody pay.[12]

When we realize that powers and authorities and sinful people are to
blame, our pain and outrage and compassion for the victims rise up. It is
natural to want to make those responsible pay.

---

9. Cockburn, "Rocket Launcher."

10. World Food Programme, "Hunger." See also Bread for the World, http://www.
bread.org; Oxfam, http://oxfam.ca; and the World Health Organization, http://www.
who.int.

11. World Health Organization, "Global Health Observatory," n.p.

12. Cockburn, "Rocket Launcher."

Ah, but here we run into trouble. What does one do, after all, when the realization hits home that one of those responsible, one of the proposed targets of the rocket launcher, is . . . oneself?

That's the other, more sinister, side of our eavesdropping. Not only do we listen in on the conversations and prayers of the poor as they cry out to God for bread, but we also bear a large part of the responsibility for putting them in that dire situation in the first place. In first-century Galilee, the peasants who had lost their livelihoods and felt the constant gnawing of hunger and resentment knew where to look to lay the blame. They laid it at the feet of the wealthy landowners who had pushed them off their land. The blame also fell on the Temple hierarchy who demanded tithes. And on Herod Antipas, who sent his tax-gatherers to wring from them what little they had left. And behind them all stretched the ever-present, ever-lengthening shadow of the Roman eagle.

In the developing world in the twenty-first century, the names and faces have changed, but it's the same old story. Local thugs and warlords hold sway and use violence and threats of violence to control "their" territory. Kleptocrats enrich themselves and live in fabulous luxury after raping the land and bleeding it dry. They receive backing from multinational corporations who want access to cheap labor. These corporations hire enforcers to keep complaints to a minimum as they steal the natural resources of the region and take advantage of lax regulations on pollution and worker safety. Behind all these stretches the shadow of another eagle—a bald one. The American Empire provides the muscle and pulls the strings to open up markets, protect the multinationals, and rig the system of international trade so local farmers and manufacturers never get a chance to play on a level field with the Big Boys.

It would be unfair, I hasten to add, to ignore all the good the US does in the world. The work of the US Agency for International Development (USAID) and its partner organizations has helped millions of people not only survive catastrophes but build a solid foundation of sustainable development for the future. The President's Emergency Plan for AIDS Relief (PEPFAR), an initiative started by President George W. Bush, has saved countless lives by making antiretroviral drugs and effective prevention measures available to those hardest hit by the AIDS pandemic in sub-Saharan Africa. The Bill and Melinda Gates Foundation, World Vision, the United Nations Foundation, Samaritan's Purse, and many other charitable organizations have made tremendous strides in combating malaria and other communicable diseases, increasing girls' access to education, bringing sanitation systems and potable water to communities in need, and boosting maternal health and child survival rates throughout the developing world. What's more, these organizations make partnership a priority; they cooperate with local civil society groups, building their capacity to meet the needs in their own communities.

I also want to point out that, despite the dire statistics in this chapter, life has actually gotten better for many people in developing countries in recent decades. Consider these encouraging statistics:

- The percentage of people in developing nations living on less than $1.25 per day (the international indicator of extreme poverty) fell from 47 percent in 1990 to 22 percent in 2010.

- The percentage of chronically undernourished people in these countries dropped from 23 percent in the years 1990–92 to 15 percent in 2010–12.

- 76 percent of the world's people had access to clean water (from pipes or protected wells) in 1990. By 2012 the number had risen to 89 percent.

- In 1990, 24 percent of the world's population had no access to indoor sanitation facilities; in 2012, only 14 percent could say the same thing.

- 523,000 women in the developing world died in 1990 from complications in pregnancy and childbirth; in 2013, the number had fallen to 289,000.

- The number of children in developing nations who did not attend primary school dropped from 102 million in 2000 to 57 million in 2011.[13]

We can and should find encouragement in these trends. But we can and should also continue to strive for a world where *no one* dies of hunger, *everyone* has access to clean water and education, and so on. And we Americans must also grapple with the reality that, while we do give generously to alleviate the ills of the world, we also contribute significantly to those ills through our policies and our actions on the global stage.

Consider just one example. US agricultural subsidies in excess of $3.4 billion per year distort world markets, making it harder for poorer countries that do not subsidize their farmers to compete. In 2002, the United

13. Beiser, "Seven Big Ways."

States gave $10 million in development aid to the West African nation of Burkina Faso. In that same year, however, subsidies to American cotton growers depressed world prices so much that Burkinabe cotton farmers, who produce cotton much more efficiently than their American counterparts, lost $13.7 million in export earnings.[14] A 2004 report from Oxfam International noted, "The impact of US cotton subsidies is not simply on balance of payments or debt service. *They cause poverty*."[15] With one talon the American Eagle gives; with the other it takes away.

What gives the Eagle the impetus to keep its talons gripped so tightly on the poor of the world? One answer is our greed, wastefulness, and addiction to comfort. The US accounts for only about 4.5 percent of the world's population but consumes 19 percent of the world's energy.[16] We have come to expect the year-round availability of low-priced food and other commodities, and few of us inquire very deeply into the conditions in which those who grow and pick them live. Plus, an unconscionable amount of the food available to us gets wasted. The USDA reports that 31 percent of the food available to consumers in 2010 went uneaten. This food loss carried a price tag of $162 billion and represented a waste of 141 *trillion* calories—1,249 calories per person per day.[17]

And then there is oil. What catastrophic, unconscionable waste of resources and human lives we have blundered into because of our thirst for light, sweet crude! Our misadventures in the Middle East for fifty years and more have brought down upon us the mistrust and hate of hundreds of millions of people. We have rained down upon them bombs, invasion forces, and political chaos, all so we can feed our habit for gasoline and diesel fuel. We express outrage when the price at the pump rises a few cents, but how often do we ask after the well-being of the workers and citizens in places like Nigeria, Ecuador, and Mali when the oil companies bring their drilling equipment and pipelines into their villages and farms?

In Sydney Pollack's 1975 film *Three Days of the Condor*, Robert Redford, who plays a low-level functionary in the CIA, inadvertently uncovers a rogue operation within the agency that seems to be preparing to invade

14. Pfeifer et al., *Moral Fiber*, 2–3, 10–11.

15. Pfeifer et al., *Moral Fiber*, 3 (emphasis added).

16. For the US's share of the world's population, see WorldOMeters: Real Time World Statistics, http://www.worldometers.info/world-population. For the US's energy consumption as a percentage of the world total, see the US Energy Information Administration, http://www.eia.gov/tools/faqs/faq.cfm?id=87&t=1.

17. Buzby et al., "Postharvest Food Losses," iii.

the Middle East to secure control of oil fields. Literally out to lunch, he narrowly misses being killed when hit men take out everyone else in his office. He goes on the run for three days, desperately trying to stay alive long enough to figure out what's going on. He finally pieces it together and, in the final scene of the movie, confronts a higher-level operative, played by Cliff Robertson, with what he has learned. Robertson denies that the CIA has any concrete plans for invasion; they simply run scenarios to see what is possible: "We have games. That's all. We play games—what if? How many men? What would it take? Is there a cheaper way to destabilize a regime? That's what we're paid to do." Unfortunately, one of the operatives took the games a little too seriously, started to put the plans in motion, and was only halted when Redford started asking questions. A crucial exchange follows that speaks volumes about our complicity in others' misery:

> Robertson: Fact is, there was nothing wrong with the plan. The plan was all right. The plan would have worked.
>
> Redford: Boy, what is it with you people? You think not getting caught in a lie is the same thing as telling the truth?
>
> Robertson: No, it's simple economics. Today, it's oil, right? In ten or fifteen years—food, plutonium . . . and maybe even sooner. What do you think the people are going to want us to do then?
>
> Redford: Ask them.
>
> Robertson: Not now. Then. Ask them when they're running out. Ask them when there's no heat and they're cold. Ask them when their engines stop. Ask them when people who have never known hunger start going hungry. Want to know something? They won't want us to ask them. They'll [just] want us to get it for them.[18]

Does it bother you that, if this comes anywhere close to an accurate portrayal of what goes on in the real world (and I think it's at least in the ballpark), our government regularly commits atrocities on our behalf? That they assume we don't really want to know what it takes to keep us in comfort, as long as we stay comfortable? It bothers me. It bothers me even more that I'm not sure how I would react if suddenly *my* A/C stopped working or *my* engine wouldn't start. Would I take the sanguine view, telling myself that if most of the rest of the world could get along without these things, so could I? Or have my addictions to the comforts and luxuries I enjoy grown

18. "Telling Stories," *Three Days of the Condor*, 1975.

so strong that I would want someone to do something, *anything*, to get me what I needed to maintain my habit? It's an unsettling question, but one that we need to wrestle with. Perhaps if we took the question seriously, and admitted our uncertainty about the answer, it would be the first step on the path to a deeper commitment to simple living and to seeking justice and equity for *all* of God's children.

"Give us tomorrow's bread today," when the poor pray it, expresses trust and confidence in God, even when things look bleakest. It voices a heartfelt cry of need from those who know what it means to live hand to mouth, day by day. It is a modest request: "Let me have the peace of mind of knowing I'll have something to feed my children tomorrow. Just get me through another day." One finds trust in this prayer of the poor, and expectation, and a mild flavor of desperation. At its core, though, it is a prayer of radical faith.

For rich eavesdroppers, however, who have never *really* felt the need to trust God for the basic necessities of life, it is none of these things. For us, it can become a hollow plea we say merely because it is part of the script. If we really take to heart all that Jesus wants to teach us through this model prayer, the petition can come to have a new and powerful meaning. For the rich, "Give us tomorrow's bread today" must become a prayer of repentance. Each time we utter those words, we should confess that we have participated in and benefited from systems that have lifted us up by grinding our sisters and brothers into the dirt. And because true repentance has little to do with sorrowful feelings but much to do with changed behaviors, this petition must become a rallying cry that leads into action, sacrifice, and sharing. It must serve as our pledge to work for the changes that have to take place if God's kingdom is to come and God's will is to be done on earth. Here. Now.

When no one on earth has to pray this prayer with desperation any longer; when everyone has enough food and no longer feels the gnawing pain of either hunger or insecurity; when everyone in the world enjoys access to clean water, medicine, sanitation, and safety; when all people can, in the words of the prophet, "sit under their own vines and under their own fig trees, and no one shall make them afraid" (Mic 4:4), then and only then will we have learned to pray the Lord's Prayer as Jesus intended. Then and only then will we learn the *other* meaning of "tomorrow's bread."

It could be that Jesus has in mind not only tomorrow as in the day after today, but also tomorrow as in the eschatological Day of the Lord. In that case, "tomorrow's bread" would be the great banquet in the kingdom of God—a banquet with room at the table for everyone. A banquet where the ones who have suffered most will sit in the places of highest honor. A banquet characterized by sharing and reconciliation and, above all, joy.

Amen. Come quickly, Lord Jesus, and bring us tomorrow's bread today.

5

Jubilee!

. . . and forgive us our debts,
as we forgive our debtors.

WHEN JESUS INSTRUCTS HIS disciples to pray for God's kingdom to come and God's will to be done *on earth* as in heaven, he gives us a clue about how to interpret the Prayer, the Sermon on the Mount, and, in fact, his entire mission. Jesus carried out an earthly mission, and he concerned himself with earthly matters at least as much as heavenly or spiritual ones. Or, better, he understood the absolute inseparability of the earthly and the heavenly, and gave attention to the latter through his focus on the former. Jesus took a realistic look at what was happening to the poorest and most vulnerable among his people, and in his passion for God and his righteous indignation at evil and injustice, he developed a strategy to redress these wrongs.

This strategy involved creative non-cooperation with evil (see his teachings about turning the left cheek, walking the second mile, and sur-rendering one's tunic when sued for one's cloak).[1] It relied on a remarkably

---

1. These teachings appear, in slightly different forms, in Matthew 5:38–42 and Luke 6:27–30. The conventional interpretation suggests that Jesus counseled acquiescence to evil, and for that reason these instructions have become widely considered irrelevant, unsatisfactory, or even counterproductive. In contrast, Walter Wink sees Jesus's teachings

humanistic interpretation of the Torah (see his teachings and actions related to the Sabbath and the dietary laws).[2] And it sought to create a radically egalitarian community that rejected patriarchy and status distinctions.[3] This countercultural strategy defied social and religious conventions right and left. In doing so, it made enemies of the traditional custodians of power, such as the priests and guardians of the Temple state. As an economic and political strategy, it empowered the impoverished and marginalized by creating a community based on the sharing of resources, mutuality in suffering, and defiance of the powers.

Jesus was, in essence, a community organizer. He sought to help the Galilean peasantry recover their dignity and discover their power. His efforts were energized and sustained by his prophetic vision of a world characterized by equity, reconciliation, and justice—a world he described as the kingdom of God.

DOCETISM 2.0

I realize many readers will be disturbed, even outraged, by this description of Jesus's work. "You're putting the cart before the horse," I can hear them

---

about turning the other cheek, going the second mile, and giving up one's tunic when sued for one's cloak as elements in a strategy of creative, nonviolent resistance to oppression and injustice. In the example of the cheek, Matthew's version specifies that the first blow has fallen on the *right* cheek, indicating a backhanded slap of the kind meant to humiliate a person of lower social status and to "put him in his place." In Jesus's creative solution, the peasant, instead of offering the expected response of groveling or backing down, asserts his dignity by offering his *left* cheek to be struck as well. This presents the slapper with a dilemma: because it was a cultural taboo to use one's left hand except for unclean tasks, he must decide if he wants to escalate the incident by using a forehand slap or a punch, or save face by backing down himself. Since he did not intend to start a fistfight, but only to intimidate or humiliate the other person, he will likely choose the latter, and the "slappee" will have turned the tables on his oppressor without resorting to violence. Wink offers similar interpretations of Jesus's counsel about the second mile and the tunic, and in each case he sees him offering a clever strategy of nonviolent resistance. Mahatma Gandhi and Martin Luther King Jr. used similar tactics to expose the violence behind the British Empire and the segregated South, thereby helping their people rediscover their own sense of self-worth, self-determination, and dignity. See *Engaging the Powers*, 175–184.

2. See, for example, Mark 2:23–3:5 and parallels; John 5:1–18; and Mark 7:14–23 and parallels.

3. See, for example, Matt 23:8–12; Mark 3:31–35 and parallels; Luke 14:7–14; and Mark 9:33–35 and parallels.

say. "Jesus came to save us from our sins. He wasn't concerned primarily, if at all, about economics or politics. He had a spiritual mission, and he cared most deeply for the individual's soul. He came to die on the cross so that we could be saved and go to heaven when we die." Many Christians have a deep-seated antipathy toward the interpretation of Jesus's mission that I outlined above, as though feeding a body were somehow less important or less holy than feeding a soul. They seem to think it would somehow cheapen the meaning of Jesus if we brought him down into the mundane affairs of life, instead of letting him glide along on some "higher" spiritual plane.

My response to these objections is that they are—well, wrong. One of the earliest Christian heresies—so early that we find mention of it in the New Testament (primarily in the three epistles of John, which were probably written in the 90s or around the turn of the second century)—was known as *docetism*. The name derives from *dokeo*, a Greek word meaning to "seem" or "appear." The docetists had undoubtedly bought into one of the Greek philosophical schools that classified the physical world as evil and the spiritual as pure, and therefore had real problems with the Incarnation. They found the claim that the Word had become flesh (John 1:14) abhorrent, so they came up with a convenient solution: Jesus had only *appeared* to be a real, physical human being. In actuality, he was pure spirit. At the crucifixion, God replaced Jesus with someone else (sort of like substitutionary atonement in reverse), thereby protecting him from the indignity of suffering and death.

It would seem that today's church is riddled with modern-day docetists who see Jesus as some magical figure—a wonder-worker whose feet never really touched the ground. These contemporary docetists don't deny the reality of Jesus's suffering; in fact, for some of them, more suffering adds greater potency to the redemption Jesus's death effected (consider the unrelenting gore of Mel Gibson's *The Passion of the Christ*). But they engage in another form of denial that may be just as, if not more, dangerous: they deny that Jesus's death was the consequence of natural, human, political forces. For them, God ordained Jesus to die before God created the world, and his only real purpose in living was to die in our place so that we might be saved.[4] These new docetists likewise imagine salvation

4. Persons who hold to this view appeal to a phrase that appears in Revelation 13:8 (see also 1 Peter 1:19–20): "the Lamb who was slain from the creation of the world" (TNIV). They claim that this means God had the intention of sending Jesus to redeem the world from its sin before any sin had yet been committed—from before creation

in strictly spiritual, individualistic terms. Jesus saves our souls from the consequences of our sinful nature, and salvation means, above all else, that we will now spend eternity in a blissful heaven rather than roasting in hell as we deserve.

Docetic Christians prefer to interpret Jesus's life, teachings, and healings in overly spiritualized ways as well. For them, Jesus cared most about how people responded to him: did they accept or reject him as the Son of God?[5] He delivered his sermons, parables, and discourses, and performed his healings and other "miracles" for the purpose of raising the question of acceptance or rejection in their minds. It is patently obvious, given this understanding, that an interpretation such as the one I offered above is unworthy of Jesus Christ, the Son of God. Why would the Savior of the World remotely concern himself with something so mundane and trifling as his disciples' real estate problems when he had so much bigger and more

---

began, in fact. If, however, we understand kosmos, (world), the way I describe it above, as equivalent to the Domination System, we get a completely different interpretation. This reading suggests that Jesus's redemptive act on the cross became a foregone conclusion from the time, eons ago in human prehistory, that the Domination System, with its myth of redemptive violence and its glorification of power-over, arose. In other words, God did not ordain from the beginning of time that Jesus should die as a sacrifice because of some eternal divine insistence on atonement through blood. Rather, Jesus's death became inevitable from the moment the Domination System began to hold sway, because, in his mission to free people from their enslavement to that System, it was completely certain that he would run afoul of the System's guardians, and that they would respond the only way they knew how: with violent repression. The key to our redemption was that he did not return violence for violence. Instead, "Jesus *absorbed* all the violence directed at him by people and by the Powers and still loved them," as Walter Wink puts it (*Engaging the Powers*, 152, emphasis added). Thus, Jesus's death need not be seen as eternally foreordained to satisfy God's bloodlust, but as the predictable consequence of the bloodlust that typifies the Domination System, and the atonement his death affords comes from his breaking the spiral of violence, not by his serving as a substitutionary sacrifice to save us from God's wrath. The powers, not God, necessitated Jesus's sacrifice, and his death revealed God's love and nonviolent nature, not God's wrath.

5. Only in the gospel of John does Jesus seem concerned with people's response to him personally—see, for example, John 3:13–18, 3:36, 5:22–24, and 6:29—but John writes in a very different context than the other Evangelists. His is the latest gospel, and he writes in the midst of a fierce controversy between Jews who accept Jesus as Messiah and those who do not. Historically, this controversy marks the beginning of the rupture between what would become rabbinic Judaism and what would become Christianity—a rupture that persists to this day. John writes in a polemical manner, and places Jesus in situations that more accurately reflect his own circumstances at the turn of the second century than the circumstances of Jesus in the late 20s. For a masterful interpretation of the gospel from this perspective, see Martyn, *History and Theology*.

cosmic fish to fry? Docetic Christians believe it is important to give a starving person food to help him survive, but it is far more important to feed his soul. For some, giving someone food without also giving him a chance to receive Christ into his heart is a missed opportunity, if not an actual sin. Evangelism is a race against the clock; we must lead these poor benighted souls to accept Jesus into their hearts so that when they do ultimately die, they will go to heaven, which is all that ultimately matters.

The Christians who hold these views would do well to remember what the writer of the Johannine epistles called the docetists of his day. He called them *antichrist* (1 John 4:2–3; see also 2 John 7). When we hear the word "antichrist," our minds automatically run to the apocalyptic. We think of the *Left Behind* books, or movies such as *The Omen*, or the rantings and PowerPoint slides of one of those "end-times prophets" so prominent on cable TV or the Internet. But that's not what John had in mind then, nor do I have it in mind now. The spirit of antichrist that plagues the church today is much more subtle and in some ways far more dangerous than those imagined fiends. Our modern-day docetists pose a fearful danger because their over-spiritualization of Jesus anesthetizes us and threatens to render Jesus's vision of the kingdom of God a quixotic, otherworldly, and ultimately irrelevant pipe dream. This becomes clear when we consider the next petition in the Lord's Prayer.

TRESPASSES VS. DEBTS

"Forgive us our trespasses, as we forgive those who trespass against us," many of us pray every Sunday. But the Lord's Prayer, as it appears in the gospel of Matthew, says nothing about trespasses. It speaks of *debts*: "Forgive us our debts [Gk. *opheilemata*], as we forgive our debtors." Some churches use this debts/debtors version as their preferred form for public recitation of the Prayer. But for a considerable majority of English-speaking Christian congregations throughout the world, trespasses have replaced debts.

Actually, the version of the Prayer we find in the gospel of Luke uses a different word altogether. In Luke 11:4 we read, "Forgive us our sins [Gk *hamartias*], for we also forgive everyone who sins against us" (TNIV). The original version of the Prayer appeared in the Q gospel, the hypothetical source of the sayings that Matthew and Luke have in common but that do not appear in Mark. Since one can easily read debts metaphorically as sins, but finds it a much less natural transition to go from sins to literal debts, it makes sense to suppose that the prayer in Q used the word for debts. In *The Greatest Prayer*, John Dominic Crossan demonstrates that former transition—from literal debts to metaphorical trespasses or sins— in Matthew and Luke, and concludes that Jesus had in mind literal debts when he taught the disciples the Prayer. He writes, "Were it originally and clearly metaphorical—'debts' meaning 'sins'—everyone would have understood that intention and the progression in terminology from 'debts' to 'trespasses' to 'sins' would not have been necessary." At the same time, Crossan suggests that the very presence of that progression from debts to sins means that both ideas are important. He says, "It seems advisable to read Matthew's text as including *both* debt *and* sin—not debt alone, not sin alone, and certainly not sin instead of debt, but both together."[6] But since the overwhelming preponderance of commentary and reflection on this petition throughout the history of Christian thought has been on the side of the metaphorical reading, in this chapter I will pay primary attention to the literal one, and focus on the forgiveness of real-world monetary debts.

I consider it important to make this small gesture toward correcting the imbalance because the habit of spiritualizing everything Jesus ever said or did has become practically an automatic reflex for many in the church. It's that docetic urge—Jesus couldn't have been talking about monetary debts; he only *seemed* to be. He used the language of debts as a metaphor for the spiritual reality of the sin that separates us from God. According to hard-core modern docetism, Jesus offers up a prayer for which he himself is the answer. After all, what brings about forgiveness of our sin-debt if not Jesus's death on the cross? And why would the answer to the sin problem for the whole world bother with run-of-the-mill literal debts?

To answer that question we must return once more to the Incarnation, which, as we have seen, represented the primary stumbling block for the original docetists. Jesus really was a flesh-and-blood human being who experienced human relationships and had to deal with real human problems. Problems such as finding a way to feed himself and his family, paying his taxes, meeting his religious obligations, and, yes, repaying his debts or forgiving debts owed to him. The people he addressed in the Sermon on the Mount and in his parables likewise knew intimately these and other mundane issues of survival in a world where the cards seemed perpetually stacked against them.

6. Crossan, *The Greatest Prayer*, 160 (emphasis in the original).

I suspect that the ascendancy of trespasses over debts happened because of the docetic church's discomfiture with this picture of Jesus as an ordinary peasant trying to get by in a subsistence culture. And now this new brand of docetism, combined with the affluence and dominance of first-world Christians, seeks to confine Jesus to the heaven ghetto by interpreting both trespasses and debts in the most spiritualized, otherworldly way possible.

If we really want to take Jesus seriously, we have to stop doing that. Jesus taught his disciples to pray for the forgiveness of debts. Let's see what happens if we take that as literally as possible.

THE SPIRIT OF JUBILEE

The idea of debt forgiveness did not originate with Jesus. He was tugging on a thread that runs all the way back through the wisdom literature and the prophets to the indisputable core of the Hebrew Scriptures, the Torah. This thread is the bedrock conviction that God is the true king of Israel and the true owner of the land. Over and over again throughout the Torah we hear the refrain, "I am the LORD your God, who brought you out of Egypt," or simply, "I am the LORD." This is God's shorthand way of reminding the people that until God had intervened, they had been slaves in a foreign country, and only by God's grace and steadfast love were they now free and on their way to the land God—the liberating God whose name is YHWH—promised to their ancestors. God, therefore, gets to make the rules. What they may eat, when they may or may not work, how they are to worship, and more are all subject to God's approval.

This theme of God's sovereignty and ownership gets expressed in a practical and, for our discussion, very pertinent way in the concept of the sabbatical year. Just as God sets aside the seventh day of the week as a day of rest for the Israelites and their slaves and animals, God also has some special provisions in mind for the seventh year.

First, God designs the sabbatical year as a year of *rest*, but this time for the land itself. For six years the Israelites may plant, cultivate, and harvest their crops as usual, but in the seventh the land must lie fallow. They may eat what grows on its own that year, but they may not work the land at all. Since that time we have learned the agricultural value of crop rotation and fallow seasons for the replenishment of the soil, nitrogen fixation, and so on, but here we have a far more radical idea than that. God asserts ownership of the land and sovereignty over the people, and demands a response of both obedience and radical faith. The people must trust God to provide for them plentifully enough in the sixth year to carry them through until the eighth year's harvest. God says, "Trust me, and I will bless you and take care of you." But God also says, "Do it because I told you to. It's my land and I get to set the rules."

Second, the seventh year is a year of *liberty*. Israelites who have fallen on hard times and sold themselves into slavery must be released in the sabbatical year without any payment or other compensation. Their owners may not simply cut them loose to fend for themselves, however. God says, "When you release them, do not send them away empty-handed. Supply them liberally from your flock, your threshing floor, and your winepress. Give to them as the LORD your God has blessed you" (Deut 15:13–14 TNIV). The rationale for this command? "Remember that you were slaves in Egypt and the LORD your God redeemed you" (Deut 15:15 TNIV). The land is mine, you are mine, and all that you have has come from me, so don't act as if this is a hardship.

A third element of the sabbatical year involves the canceling of *debts*. God forbids the people to charge interest on loans to their fellow Israelites in the first place (Lev 25:36); on top of that, God tells them to forgive all outstanding debts when the seventh year rolls around (Deut 15:1). And because God knows how our petty, mean little minds work, God warns the creditors against being tight-fisted and refusing to lend to their neighbors as the sabbatical year draws near (Deut 15:9). God commands generosity and forgiveness of debts—actual, real-life debts, not just spiritual or moral ones—and God's sovereignty and ownership once again forms the basis for the command.

Whenever this subject comes up, the objections start flying. That's bad fiscal policy! It punishes thrift! It rewards laziness and waste! You can't expect a sensible businessperson to follow these rules! No interest? Who are you trying to kid?

These objections fail to acknowledge, however, that God shows no concern at all for sensible or successful business practices. God cares about justice. As hard to believe as it may be for those of us who have been indoctrinated to equate "God's will" and "the American way," God is not a capitalist. Many of the structures on which our system relies for its very existence, such as compound interest, planned obsolescence, rampant consumerism, the primacy of competition, an economics of credit and debt,

and fabricated demand—things we might call good business—God calls
by different names. Greed. Ingratitude. Selfishness. Predation. God intends
the instructions regarding debt forgiveness, the release of slaves, and the
rest not for the good of the debtor and the slave only. God knows that the
slaveholder and the creditor benefit from these rules as well, because they
help to safeguard or restore their sense of community, mutuality, and humanity. Capitalism is the enemy of all these. Unrestrained capitalism iso-
lates and dehumanizes the haves as much as or more than the have-nots.
God's rules bring us back into proper relationship with God, each other,
and our possessions. When we recognize God as our sovereign and the
owner of all, it brings everything else into its proper perspective.

This brings us to the final element in our exploration of these related
themes from the Torah: the year of jubilee. Only in the twenty-fifth chapter
of Leviticus do we find this particular term, but the spirit of jubilee infuses
all other instances of liberation related to the sabbatical year. As a result,
"jubilee" has become a sort of shorthand for all manner of liberating and re-
newing events. From the emancipation of American slaves, to the collapse
of the Iron Curtain, to the campaign to forgive foreign debt, to efforts to
ensure and protect religious freedom, to the push for nuclear disarmament,
jubilee has become a watchword and a rallying cry.

In its origins, the year of jubilee had to do with restoration and freedom for the poor among the Israelites. Leviticus 25 tells the people to count
off seven sabbatical years—seven times seven years, or forty-nine years—
and in the fiftieth year to celebrate the jubilee. A trumpet blast on the Day
of Atonement (Yom Kippur) signals the start of the commemoration, and
announces freedom to the enslaved and good news to the poor.

In the year of jubilee, all the Israelites are to return to their ancestral
lands. Even if during the intervening fifty years they have become impoverished and had to sell their land, or even had to sell themselves into slavery,
they are to return in the jubilee year. God exercises the prerogative to allot
the land to whomever God chooses: "The land must not be sold permanently, because the land is mine, and you reside in my land as foreigners
and strangers. Throughout the land that you hold as a possession, you must
provide for the redemption of the land" (Lev 25:23–24 TNIV). The land can
be redeemed at any time by either the poor person's nearest kin or by the
person himself, if he has prospered, but in the year of jubilee the land is to
revert to its original holder, regardless of his ability to pay.

Again, those of us for whom capitalism has been like mother's milk find this grossly unfair to the buyer. As long as the owner has not swindled anyone and bought the land fair and square, he should get to keep it until such time as he sees fit to sell it. What right does anyone have to take it away? The answer, familiar enough by now, comes back that God has that right because God has held the deed to the land all along.

God means for the year of jubilee and the other provisions of the sabbatical year to serve as equalizers. Call it a redistribution of wealth, if you will. No one is to become too poor or too rich, and no one is to gain a permanent advantage over his neighbor. Every seventh or fiftieth year, the slate gets cleaned—debts get canceled, slaves go free, and land ownership goes back to square one. God owns the land, God rules the people, and God cares for everyone equally. The story of the Exodus tells us, and the Hebrew prophets and Jesus reaffirm again and again, that God is a God of liberation, renewal, justice, and grace. The spirit of jubilee dances cheek-to-cheek with the Spirit of God.

IGNORING JUBILEE

It has become commonplace in biblical criticism to point out that no hard evidence exists within Scripture or without to suggest that the ancient Israelites ever enacted the jubilee provisions. They may therefore express nothing more than an impractical, utopian ideal that never saw the light of day. This strikes me as rather disingenuous, and sounds suspiciously like rich first-worlders' efforts to justify themselves and their lifestyles. We have no hard evidence that the death penalty was ever carried out against men who had sexual relations with other men, but that has not stopped many Christian leaders from citing Leviticus 20:13 in their crusade against the LGBT community. It seems we choose to emphasize those parts of Scripture that fit our worldview or serve our interests and downplay those that go against them. We all do it from time to time and need to ask the Spirit of God to help us rise above this self-serving tendency.

Whether or not jubilee was ever officially enacted, we find the *expectation* of jubilee throughout both the Old and New Testaments. Consider these examples:

> If the people of the land bring in merchandise or any grain on the sabbath day to sell, we will not buy it from them on the sabbath or

on a holy day; and we will forego the crops of the seventh year and the exaction of every debt (Neh 10:31 TNIV).

The spirit of the Lord GOD is upon me,
  because the LORD has anointed me;
he has sent me to bring good news to the oppressed,
  to bind up the brokenhearted,
to proclaim liberty to the captives,
  and release to the prisoners;
to proclaim the year of the Lord's favor,
  and the day of vengeance of our God (Isa 61:1–2; see also Luke 4:18–19).

King Zedekiah had made a covenant with all the people in Jerusalem to make a proclamation of liberty to them—that all should set free their Hebrew slaves, male and female, so that no one should hold another Judean in slavery. And they obeyed (Jer 34:8–10 TNIV).

The prince shall not take any of the inheritance of the people, thrusting them out of their holding; he shall give his sons their inheritance out of his own holding, so that none of my people shall be dispossessed of their holding (Ezek 46:18 TNIV).

Jesus spoke up and said to him, "Simon, I have something to say to you." "Teacher," he replied, "Speak." "A certain creditor had two debtors; one owed five hundred denarii, and the other fifty. When they could not pay, he canceled the debts for both of them. Now which of them will love him more?" Simon answered, "I suppose the one for whom he canceled the greater debt." And Jesus said to him, "You have judged rightly" (Luke 7:40–43).

The themes of liberation, debt forgiveness, and the inviolability of one's ancestral land holdings are woven throughout the Scriptures in such a way that we can recognize the people's expectation of these things. With the God of Israel, one can count on justice, equity, and restoration.

Unfortunately, not everyone got the memo. Another thread that runs through the Bible is the way some tried to get around these rules so they could gain an advantage over others. People don't change much—then, as now, they looked for loopholes. They observed the letter of the law but mangled its spirit. Because of avarice, insecurity, and predatory instincts, they sought to amass more and more riches, even if it meant the vast majority of their fellows had to make do with less and less. Then, as now, some people became quite adept at ignoring jubilee.

The archetypal story from the Old Testament is that of Naboth's vine-yard. Ahab, the king of Israel, looks out of the window of his palace in the city of Jezreel one day and sees a vineyard belonging to his neighbor Naboth, sitting precisely where Ahab's vegetable garden needs to be. So he goes to Naboth and offers to buy his vineyard. He offers him a good price or a comparable trade. A very reasonable request, Ahab thinks—a win–win—but Naboth refuses to sell.

Naboth explains that the vineyard grows on land that forms part of his ancestral holding, and for him to sell off part of his inheritance would be both an insult to his forebears and a sin against God. I agree, it's a very generous offer, Naboth says, but my hands are tied. It's the Law, after all. My answer is no.

King Ahab has little experience in being refused, but he can't see any way around the Law, so he goes home and pouts. His wife Jezebel, on the other hand, hails from a foreign land and has no reverence for the Torah, or the principle of jubilee, or even God. But she is the daughter of a king, so she does know something about getting what she wants. After upbraid-ing her husband for his unkingly behavior, she sets in motion a nefarious scheme. She gets false witnesses to accuse Naboth of treason and blasphe-my, which leads to Naboth's execution. She then goes to Ahab and tells him that the vineyard has suddenly and unexpectedly come back on the market, and that he should go plant his vegetables. Ahab stops sulking, wipes his nose, and goes to take possession of Naboth's vineyard. They have clearly violated the Law and the spirit of jubilee, and the prophet Elijah announces God's displeasure by predicting violent deaths for Ahab, Jezebel, and all of Ahab's male descendants, effectively ending his dynasty. All these predic-tions come true within a dozen years.

Whether God did in fact exact violent revenge on Ahab's family, or the biblical writers interpreted their fates as God's judgment after the fact, I will leave it to you to decide for yourself. In either case, however, we see clearly in this story that at least some in Israelite society took God's ownership of the land and the spirit of jubilee quite seriously.

The writings of the prophets also contain evidence of the Israelites' habit of ignoring jubilee. Consider these scathing critiques from Amos, Micah, and Isaiah:

> Hear this, you that trample on the needy, and bring to ruin the poor of the land, saying, "When will the new moon be over so that we may sell grain; and the sabbath, so that we may offer wheat

for sale? We will make the ephah small and the shekel great, and
practice deceit with false balances, buying the poor for silver and
the needy for a pair of sandals, and selling the sweepings of the
wheat." The LORD has sworn by the pride of Jacob: Surely I will
never forget any of their deeds (Amos 8:4–7).

Alas for those who devise wickedness and evil deeds on their beds!
When the morning dawns, they perform it, because it is in their
power. They covet fields, and seize them; houses, and take them
away; they oppress householder and house, people and their inheritance (Mic 2:1–2).

Ah, you who join house to house,
  who add field to field,
until there is room for no one but you,
  and you are left to live alone in the midst of the land!
The LORD of hosts has sworn in my hearing:
  Surely many houses shall be desolate,
  large and beautiful houses, without inhabitant (Isa 5:8–9).

We see in these examples violations of both the spirit and the letter
of the law of jubilee. We also see how God feels about such violations, and
how God vows to respond to those who insist on ignoring jubilee.

Keeping in mind all this context, let us turn again to the petition,
"Forgive us our debts as we forgive our debtors." As we have seen, Jesus
taught this prayer to poor, marginalized, and disenfranchised Galilean
peasants. He didn't need to explain to them the significance of a prayer for
the remission of debts, or the longing for a return of the spirit of jubilee that
this prayer evokes. Many of them—perhaps most of them, perhaps Jesus
himself—had direct experience with crushing debt and its consequences:
foreclosure, loss of one's ancestral inheritance, even debt slavery. For them,
this prayer was not only a request for God to forgive their trespasses on the
spiritual plane, but also a defiant, even angry, call for God to redress their
real-world grievances. A cry for political, social, and economic liberation,
as well as the spiritual liberation that goes along with them. We focus on the
spiritual to the exclusion of the other aspects of liberation only at our peril.

A CASE STUDY

To understand the circumstances and social location of these people better,
we may find it helpful to consider a hypothetical case study. Let us imagine

a Galilean peasant whom we will call Elihu. As our story begins, Elihu owns a modest parcel of land—less than four acres, but he takes great pride in it because it has been in his family for many generations. On it he grows wheat, millet, barley, and lentils; raises a few sheep; and tends a small grove of olive trees. Everything is fine until the drought hits. The farms of the wealthy landowner that adjoin his property survive pretty well, because this neighbor has access to the aqueduct and can keep his crops irrigated throughout even the driest months of the growing season. Elihu and the other small freeholders in the vicinity can't afford the fees or bribes necessary to have water diverted to their fields, so they reap a meager harvest and cannot feed their families without borrowing from their well-to-do neighbor. Or, more precisely, their neighbor's agent, or steward, as the owner actually lives in a sprawling lakeside villa in the city of Tiberias.

Elihu must borrow in order to get his family through the winter without starving, and in the spring he must borrow seed to do his planting. Now the landowner—we'll call him Alexander—has his hooks in him. Elihu has no leverage with which to bargain and must accept the terms Alexander sets for the loan. The terms are by no means generous, but not severe, either. Alexander doesn't want to appear mercenary, or to provoke undue resentment and hostility on the part of his unfortunate neighbors. He wants them to view him as a square-dealer who wishes to help out, but not such a soft touch that he will hesitate to charge a few points of interest. Besides, he is a patient man. Elihu and his neighbors don't need to know that he and the owners of the other three large estates in the area, with King Herod Antipas as their patron, control the aqueduct and the fees for use of its water. He thinks it prudent to keep that information under wraps.

Elihu feels grateful to have a benefactor, and he does his spring planting in the confident hope that with a couple of good harvests he'll be back on his feet, and free and clear of his debt.

No matter how generous Alexander may appear, however, the same cannot be said for Herod and his corrupt and widely abhorred tax-gatherers. Galilee is a client kingdom of the Roman Empire, and must pay annual tribute to Caesar in order to maintain a degree of freedom and self-rule. From his headquarters in Tiberias on the southwestern shore of the Sea of Galilee, Herod oversees the collection of a portion of each year's harvest to go to Rome. As long as he delivers the required tribute—a quarter of the harvest every second year—the Romans don't much care how he goes about it. So Herod instructs his tax-gatherers to collect 12.5 percent each year to satisfy the Roman tribute, plus another portion in taxes and "administrative fees" for his own coffers. He also gives them permission to add a little more for themselves, as a bonus for their valuable service in this thankless undertaking. For Elihu and his fellow peasants, this amounts to a double serving of taxes with a side order of extortion. Add to this the Temple tithe every adult Jewish male must pay each year, and the end result is that Elihu can't repay his loan to Alexander regardless of how good a harvest he brings in. If his crop comes in less than he expects, he may not even be able to make payments against the interest, and will almost certainly have to go back to Alexander for additional assistance.

You can see where this is going. Each year Elihu, despite his best efforts, slips a little farther behind. Before long, he is into Alexander for more than he can ever reasonably hope to pay. Another subpar year or two, and he owes more than his farm is worth. If another drought comes along, it won't even take that long.

Now Alexander starts reeling in his fish. He calls in the loan, knowing full well that Elihu can't pay it. In his great "mercy," he offers to buy Elihu's children as indentured servants. Slaves, really. The sons can be put to work in Alexander's fields. Elihu's daughter will work in the house, and will likely find herself at the mercy of her new master's appetites. If Elihu goes along with this deal, he can buy himself a few more years of relative autonomy. If he refuses, Alexander will be "forced" to foreclose. "I'm sorry, Elihu. I want to help you out here, but you're not making it easy. This recession has hit us all pretty hard, and my hands are tied. Here's what I can do for you, though. . . . "

Alexander then offers Elihu a deal. He will take the deed of the farm, but he'll keep Elihu and his sons on to work it for him. They know the land, after all, and this way they can stay in their house. So Elihu becomes a sharecropper on land his ancestors held for three centuries or longer. It brings shame to him and his family, but he has few other options.

Of course, the cycle of tribute and taxation does not stop, and now Elihu has fewer of his own resources to meet his obligations. He must continue to borrow from Alexander, digging the hole deeper and deeper until he becomes, for all intents and purposes, a debt slave. When his usefulness is played out, Alexander either kicks him off his land or reduces him to the status of a hired laborer. Or he may sell Elihu and his family into slavery, liquidate his assets, and tear down his house. In the course of a few short years, he has completely swallowed up Elihu's land, and chewed up and spat out Elihu and his family.

Multiply this scenario by the hundreds or thousands, and you have a fairly accurate picture of what Jesus faced when he left his home and family to become an itinerant preacher, exorcist, and community organizer in the late twenties in the region around the Sea of Galilee. His society teetered on the brink. Perhaps not the brink of armed rebellion, for this was actually a period of relative calm. The references to Zealots and insurrections we find in the gospels are almost certainly anachronisms, drawn from the time of the Jewish war in the late sixties.[7] (The Evangelists regularly imported themes and events from their own time into their stories of Jesus's mission.) But his society was certainly on the brink of economic disaster. The situation had become unsustainable, to say the least, and by their predatory economic practices the elites were in fact planting the seeds of revolution.

Those seeds would bloom four decades later, when the desperate and ultimately doomed Jewish War broke out in 66 CE. The uprising was directed at the hated Roman overlords, but their proxies, the aristocratic and priestly collaborators, received their due attention as well. It is not insignificant that when the rebels took control of Jerusalem in the early months of the war and killed or expelled the Roman troops there, they made it one of their first orders of business to storm the Upper City and destroy the archives that held all the land and debt records.[8] Against their will, a great many creditors did indeed forgive their debtors that summer.

---

7. For an enlightening discussion of the various groups active in Palestine from Jesus's day through the period of the Jewish War, see Horsley, *Bandits, Prophets, and Messiahs*, written with John S. Hanson.

8. Josephus, who came from the aristocratic class and held the rebels in contempt, describes the scene this way: "The king's soldiers . . . were driven out of the upper city by force. The others then set fire to the house of Ananias the high priest, and to the palaces of [King] Agrippa and [his sister] Bernice; after which they carried the fire to the place where the archives were reposited, and made haste to burn the contracts belonging to their creditors, and thereby dissolve their obligations for paying their debts; and this was done, in order to gain the multitude of those who had been debtors, and that they might persuade the poorer sort to join in their insurrection with safety against the more wealthy; so the keepers of the records fled away, and the rest set fire to them" (*War* 2.17.6).

A PROGRAM OF FORGIVENESS

Jesus did not have violent insurrection and forced debt-remission in mind, however, in the Lord's Prayer. When he looked into the desperate faces of his impoverished neighbors, he saw the rage that seethed just below the surface—rage, or at least indignation, that he likely shared. But instead of calling for violence and destruction, Jesus opted for an infinitely more positive and constructive approach. He opted for a program of forgiveness.

Jesus taught his new community to pray, "Forgive us our debts, as we forgive our debtors." For that prayer to have any force or validity, those praying had to have already embarked on the difficult path of debt forgiveness themselves. What follows is conjecture, but educated conjecture pieced together from clues scattered throughout the gospels and the book of Acts.

We find the first clue to this strategy in Jesus's parables. Like many of his other teachings—aphorisms, sermons, and so on—the parables often deal with the theme of reversal. We think of his justly famous line, "The last will be first and the first will be last" (Matt 20:16), or of a story like the one about the rich man and the beggar Lazarus. In this story Abraham tells the rich man suffering in the flames after his death, "Child, remember that during your lifetime you received your good things, and Lazarus in like manner evil things; but now he is comforted here, and you are in agony" (Luke 16:25).

Some of Jesus's sayings and parables of reversal feature themes of jubilee. One of these has become known as the parable of the unmerciful servant (see Matt 18:23–34). A slave owes his master an outrageous sum of money, the equivalent of roughly $3.5 billion today.[9] This obvious hyperbole drives home the point that the slave has no hope of ever repaying the debt. The slave throws himself on the mercy of the court, so to speak, begging his master for leniency. The master, however, does him one better (a couple *billion* better would be closer to the truth). He has compassion on the slave and forgives the entire colossal debt. Just writes it off and sends his slave home, unexpectedly free of his terrible obligation.

---

9. The parable says the amount owed was 10,000 talents. Since one talent = 6,000 denarii, and a denarius was the typical daily wage for a laborer in Jesus's time, 10,000 talents = 60,000,000 denarii. The current minimum wage in the US is $7.25 per hour. Assuming an eight-hour work day, a minimum-wage worker would make, before taxes, $58 per day. Using that amount as the rough equivalent of a denarius, 10,000 talents comes to 60,000,000 x $58 = $3,480,000,000. Using the same formula for the second debt in the parable, 100 denarii = $5,800. See Shelley, "Money," 581.

But the slave does not share his master's nobility of character. When he runs into a fellow slave who owes him a comparatively paltry sum (the equivalent of about $5,800), he refuses to listen to the other's entreaties for more time to pay. Instead, he hauls him off to the debtor's prison. Unfortunately for him, some other slaves witness this ugly scene. Aware of their master's astounding magnanimity toward this scoundrel, they find his behavior shocking and go tell the master what he has done. The master becomes understandably enraged and sends for the offender. "You wicked slave!" he says. "I forgave you all that debt because you pleaded with me. Should you not have had mercy on your fellow slave, as I had mercy on you?" (Matt 18:32–33). Without waiting for an answer, the master reinstates the slave's enormous obligation and has him thrown into debtor's prison until he repays every last penny.

We find a second clue to Jesus's program of forgiveness in a somewhat oblique reference in Mark 10 to the new community he seeks to form. It comes in the wake of Jesus's encounter with a rich man who expresses an interest in following Jesus but instead goes away disappointed. He cannot bring himself to obey Jesus's call for him to sell his possessions, give the proceeds to the poor, and then follow Jesus. Significantly, Mark says the man "had many possessions" (Mark 10:22). The Greek word for "possessions," *ktemata*, almost undoubtedly refers to land holdings, and "the poor" are the same poor, marginalized, swindled people to whom Jesus teaches the Prayer.[10] When the rich man rejects Jesus's prescription, Jesus observes, "How hard it will be for those who have wealth to enter the kingdom of God! . . . It is easier for a camel to go through the eye of a needle than for someone who is rich to enter the kingdom of God" (Mark 10:23, 25). At this, the disciples are dumfounded and ask, "Who then can be saved?" Jesus replies that with God nothing is impossible. Peter chimes in at this point, saying, "Look, we left everything to follow you," a claim that carries with it the implied question, "So what can we expect in return?"

Jesus gives what seems at first a rather cryptic response: "Truly I tell you, . . . no one who has left home or brothers or sisters or mother or father or children or fields for me and the gospel will fail to receive a hundred times as much in this present age: homes, brothers, sisters, mothers, children and fields—along with persecutions—and in the age to come eternal life" (Mark 10:29–30 TNIV). I believe Jesus here points to his new community, formed

---

10. See Myers, *Sabbath Economics*, 32–3.

on the basis of mutual sharing and a program of forgiveness. We will come back to this claim in a moment.

First, though, let us consider a third clue, this time from the book of Acts. Luke relates a set of remarkable events surrounding the coming of the Holy Spirit fifty days after the resurrection of Jesus, on the Jewish festival day of Pentecost. He then closes the second chapter of the book with this summary statement: "[The disciples] devoted themselves to the apostles' teaching and to fellowship, to the breaking of bread and to prayer. . . . All the believers were together and had everything in common. They sold property and possessions to give to anyone who had need" (Acts 2:42–45 TNIV).

After Jesus's resurrection and the outpouring of the Holy Spirit, Luke says the disciples continue to live together in Jerusalem, in a common life characterized by radical sharing. Two chapters later, we find more evidence of this communal life:

> Now the whole group of those who believed were of one heart and soul, and no one claimed private ownership of any possessions, but everything they owned was held in common. With great power the apostles gave their testimony to the resurrection of the Lord Jesus, and great grace was upon them all. There was not a needy person among them, for as many as owned lands or houses sold them and brought the proceeds of what was sold. They laid it at the apostles' feet, and it was distributed to each as any had need" (Acts 4: 32–35).

Luke goes on to report one such offering, from a disciple named Barnabas, who sells a field and shares the proceeds with the whole community.

He also relates how the system begins to break down. A couple named Ananias and Sapphira want some of the acclaim that has come Barnabas's way, so they also sell some property and bring an offering to the community. But looking to have their cake and eat it, too, they hold back some of the money for themselves and then lie to Peter when he asks about it. Both husband and wife meet sudden ends, and we hear nothing more about the radical sharing of the community of disciples in the book of Acts.

That is a bigger shame—a tragedy, even—than we may realize, because this event sets the church on a path of economic conformity that has prevailed, and at times wrought great evil, to this day. Note that the great sin of Ananias and Sapphira, a sin they pay for with their lives, springs from the greed and grasping insecurity that tells them to cling to their private property. Ironic, isn't it, that what the capitalist system, in which the contemporary first-world church lives and moves and has its being, considers an unmitigated good and an inviolable article of faith, the book of Acts depicts as a mortal sin?

Notwithstanding this tragic setback to the disciples' experiment, I see in it a direct continuation of Jesus's program from the gospels. From the first two clues we explored above, we can make a confident conjecture that the establishment of communities of radical sharing like what we see in Acts formed a large part of Jesus's mission. Richard Horsley contends that it was his entire mission. The Jesus movement, Horsley says, sought to renew the ancient covenant between Israel and God by "restor[ing] the mutuality and solidarity" within existing village communities, which "presumably would strengthen [those communities] with regard to the pressures that are contributing to [their] disintegration, most obviously the heavy taxation resulting in indebtedness . . . which exacerbates their poverty and hunger." He considers the Lord's Prayer an important component in this task. He calls it "a covenantal economic as well as religious prayer. The third petition is a combination of a plea to God for cancellation of debts and the corresponding commitment to cancel whatever debts were owed by fellow villagers. As expressed in the parallel petitions of the prayer, cancellation of debts along with the provision of subsistence food (daily bread) is what the kingdom of God means."[11]

These renewed communities shared resources, re-imagined the definition of family, and obliterated traditional social boundaries. They were utterly countercultural, which may explain why Jesus throws in the phrase "with persecutions" in his description of what the disciples could expect to gain after leaving everything to go with him. He probably considered such a radically different approach the only way to combat the corrosive and dehumanizing effects of the Domination System's economic structures. In their time, the provisions of the sabbatical year and the year of jubilee had conflicted with social norms and offered a diametrically opposed vision of wealth, property, and the allocation of resources. The Jesus movement's communities of radical sharing brought that transformative, revolutionary spirit of jubilee to their own time and place.

This explains what Jesus means when he says those who join the kingdom community receive a hundredfold in return for their sacrifice and discipleship. Everyone shares her resources in a spirit of caring and generosity. These poor downtrodden people, so powerless on their own, become rich

11. Horsley, *Jesus in Context*, 51.

when they reject the grasping competitiveness of zero-sum economics and choose instead the jubilee vision of cooperative life in community. We worship a God of abundance, and the spirit of jubilee encourages and enables us to see the world as a place of abundance and not of scarcity. An outlook of scarcity yields anxiety and competition, which in turn reinforce one's sense of scarcity, which feeds one's anxiety, and so on in an ever more dismal downward spiral. A perspective on the world as a place of abundance, on the other hand, fosters cooperation, security, and trust, which spirals up toward a realization of the reign of God.

Ched Myers puts it this way:

> In [the] conclusion to the rich man story, Mark shows that the "hundredfold" harvest promised in the sower parable (4:8) was not a pipedream offered to poor peasants, but the concrete result of wealth redistribution. This surplus is created when the entitlements of *household* (basic productive economic unit), *family* (patrimony and inheritance) and *land* (the basic unit of wealth) are . . . restructured as community assets (10:29f). "Whosoever" practices this jubilee/kingdom way will *receive* (not inherit) the community's abundant sufficiency—an allusion to the divine economy of grace. A note of realism is included: persecution will be the inevitable result of such subversive practice. The matter of eternal life, however, is left for "the age to come" (10:30).[12]

What would it mean for us to do something similar in our time and place? How would it change the way we "do church" to commit to such a countercultural community and program of forgiveness? What if we could develop a system of debt-remission and resource-sharing within autonomous groups of like-minded people? How would it change the church—how would it change our whole society—if we began living out in concrete ways this part of the Lord's Prayer? With millions of people throughout the US alone drowning in personal debt, whether from mortgages, student loans, financial setbacks, or simply from our having succumbed to the culture's insistence on perpetual consumption, Christians' implementing Jesus's program of forgiveness would have an enormous impact. To pool and share resources, to write off our debts to each other and pay off each other's debts to outside creditors, to lend money without interest—in short, to live responsibly and intentionally outside the Domination System's mechanisms of social control through indebtedness—would rock the world.

12. Myers, *Biblical Vision*, 36 (emphasis in original).

We have, in fact, numerous examples of this sort of countercultural program of forgiveness from various times and places in Christian history. The classical monastic orders, such as the Benedictines and Franciscans, included among their requirements a vow of poverty and the disavowal of private property. Churches of the Anabaptist tradition, such as the Mennonites and Amish, have long practiced communal living, mutual support, and deliberate separation from the economic and political systems of the wider world. Members of the Bruderhof give away their possessions and take lifelong vows of poverty and obedience, then work, raise their children, and care for elderly parents within the context of completely self-sufficient communities.[13] And a growing movement of intentional communities in the United States—what has been dubbed the "new monasticism"—features communal living arrangements, shared finances, and radical hospitality. These groups, such as the Rutba House and Family Tree communities in North Carolina, Reba Place Fellowship in Oregon, and the Simple Way in metro Philadelphia, differ in their structures and emphases, but each practices jubilee and a countercultural form of resistance to the Domination System.[14]

That these groups have found ways to buck the System and demonstrate the feasibility of collective Christian action encourages me greatly. To date, unfortunately, these practices have not found their way in a large scale into the church at large. What we need is a critical mass of people of faith willing to opt out of the Domination System's divide-and-conquer strategy—a significant enough minority of churches and other communities that this program of forgiveness could make a visible impact. Then, it may be said of us as it was said of the Christians in Acts, that we have turned the world upside-down (Acts 17:6).

The System wouldn't like it, of course. Any group that truly learns to live in freedom; that thumbs its nose at the System's methods and guardians; that exercises cooperation, trust, and power-with; that declares to the world that the Emperor has no clothes—any such group represents a fundamental threat to the Domination System. Are we willing to face the inevitable backlash—name-calling, punitive legislation, social ostracism,

13. Bruderhof, "The Bruderhof."

14. For an overview and analysis of these "new monastic" groups, see Byassee, "The New Monastics." For specific information on representative new monastic communities, see http://www.rebaplacefellowship.org/ (Reba Place Fellowship); http://qcfamilytree.org/ (Family Tree); http://www.thesimpleway.org/ (Simple Way); and http://emerging-communities.com/tag/rutba-house/ (Rutba House).

and so on? Are we willing to commit ourselves to this radical form of common life in the first place? Is it worth it to us? Do we care enough about the
kingdom of God to go to these lengths? The Lord's Prayer demands that we
wrestle with these questions.

Jesus taught his disciples to pray, "Forgive us our debts, as we forgive
our debtors," as a shorthand representation of the ethos of his radical jubilee communities. We can rise above the soul-crushing consequences of our
own indebtedness, poverty, and oppression, he was saying, only when we
commit ourselves wholeheartedly to a completely different set of rules. The
community could exist and thrive only when sharing was genuine, when
the cancelation of debts was mutual and total, and when every member of
the community looked after all the others with the same care as if they truly
belonged to the same family.

Which they did, of course. They had joined Jesus's reconstituted and
redefined family, which he announced when he looked around at his disciples and said, "Whoever does the will of God is my brother and sister and
mother" (Mark 3:35). He drove the point home when he taught his jubilee
communities to address their Prayer to "*Our* Father." We are all children of
one God. We are all in this together.

6

A Bigger Set of Tools

Lead us not into temptation,
but deliver us from evil.

MARK TWAIN'S SHORT STORY, "The Man That Corrupted Hadleyburg," describes a town renowned for and inordinately proud of its reputation for honesty and its self-proclaimed incorruptibility. The town motto is, "Lead us not into temptation," and the citizens do their best to avoid situations that might entice them into dishonesty or impugn their integrity in some way. They go to great lengths to shield their children from evil influences, hoping thereby to protect and preserve their innocence.

Into this ready landscape comes a stranger who takes offense at some unspecified slight by one or more of the leading citizens of Hadleyburg. Irritated by the townspeople's moral arrogance, he vows to destroy their reputation for incorruptibility. He devises an ingenious scheme to exploit the depravity he is sure lies beneath the respectable veneer of these upstanding people and to publicly expose them as hypocrites. He explains why he settled on the particular approach he uses in this way: "The weakest of all weak things is a virtue which has not been tested in the fire."[1] One of the citizens who falls victim to the stranger's scheme verifies this assessment

---

1. Twain, "Hadleyburg," 66.

from his own experience. In a conscience-stricken deathbed confession he declares, "I was clean—artificially—like the rest; and like the rest I fell when temptation came."[2] The story ends with the townspeople, chastened by their experience, changing the town motto to "Lead us *into* temptation."[3]

I often think of this story when I come to the part of the Lord's Prayer that goes, "Lead us not into temptation, but deliver us from evil." If Mark Twain knows enough about human nature to realize that an untested virtue is weak to the point of uselessness, why doesn't Jesus know this, too? Especially when you consider that just before he teaches the people this Prayer in the gospel of Matthew, he himself has endured pretty rigorous testing and temptation from no less an authority than the devil himself! How could he have got this part of the Prayer so dangerously wrong?

Or did he? Could it be instead that we have got our interpretation of this petition wrong, and that Jesus had something entirely different in mind? Let us take a closer look at the temptation petition now.

"TEMPTATION IS THAT EXTRA DESSERT"

I am just old enough to remember the *Flip Wilson Show*, which was popular in the early 1970s. One of Wilson's recurring characters used to explain her misdeeds by saying, "The devil made me do it." That is the way we often think about temptation: some evil power has enticed us and led us astray, so that we have done something we know is wrong. The infraction usually involves some personal, individual sin, such as theft, pride, lying, or lustful thoughts. This way, we can shift the responsibility for the sin away from ourselves and onto the tempter. Wilson mined this tendency of ours for laughs, but the effects of this blame game are no laughing matter.

Neither is our habit of personalizing temptation. In cartoons we depict our inner struggles with a tiny angel on one shoulder and a little demon—pitchfork, horns, and so forth—on the other. The angel represents our conscience, and usually comes off as a goody-goody character—either a killjoy or a milquetoast, and often both. The devil, on the other hand (or shoulder, to be exact), is a fun-loving, mischievous imp who wants, for whatever reason, to talk us into doing something against the rules. "Come on," he says, "it'll be fun. Don't be such a square." In the cartoons, the devil usually holds sway for a time, but the unwanted consequences of

2. Twain, "Hadleyburg," 82.

3. Twain, "Hadleyburg," 83 (emphasis added).

the person's bad behavior leads her back to the right path and the angel/ conscience wins in the end.

Cute and moralistic, this depiction trivializes the idea of temptation in a way that may become dangerous if we take it too far. In the song "It's Sick" by the seminal Christian rock band Daniel Amos, songwriter Terry Taylor bemoans the superficiality of the Christian culture in the US in the mid-1980s:

> Our trial is which car to buy;
> temptation is that extra dessert.[4]

Needless to say, Jesus did not have these kinds of trials and temptations in mind when he taught his disciples the Lord's Prayer.

As I write this, a new "meme" has appeared on the online and pop cultural landscapes that makes the same sort of point that Taylor makes in his song. It's called "First World Problems," and it refers to those kinds of petty annoyances that we in the prosperous global North face simply by virtue of the luxury in which we live. I find it an effective means of gently satirizing how spoiled we have become by excess and how seldom many of us think about the genuine life-or-death problems people in other parts of the world confront every day. In one of the best expressions of this meme that I have run across, a YouTube video shows people in the developing world quoting actual complaints from people in our part of the world. It provides a visual and ethical jolt to see a young African woman standing in front of the only working water pump in her village, with a background of blinding, sun-baked brownness, saying, "I hate it when my 4G phone will only connect to the 3G network. My downloads are *so* slow." My modest hope is that someone will see that video, recognize himself in it, and at least think twice before saying something so asinine and selfish again.

In saying all this I do not mean to characterize personal temptations as unimportant or some kind of joke. For persons with food addictions, for instance, that extra dessert presents no trivial temptation. For someone with a moral susceptibility to lust, the temptations that result from having ready access to Internet pornography are not a joke. We *do* face individual moral and ethical temptations all the time. We should take them seriously and treat those who succumb to them with grace and loving, supportive accountability, even (or especially) when the person who has succumbed is oneself. I do not wish to downplay or ridicule these very real problems. Not

---

4. Daniel Amos, "It's Sick."

at all. I simply mean Jesus may have had something else in mind—something *in addition to* these kinds of trials—when he taught us to pray, "Lead us not into temptation, but deliver us from evil."

IN CASE OF RAPTURE . . . JESUS WILL BE VERY SURPRISED

First, "temptation" is not the only possible translation of the Greek word in question, *peirasmos.* The New Revised Standard Version of the Bible translates the first part of this petition as "Do not bring us to the time of trial." Also a legitimate translation of peirasmos, "time of trial" carries with it resonances from other parts of the New Testament. The most notable examples come from the Book of Revelation and from two scenes in the gospels.

In Revelation 3:10, in a letter he dictates to the church in Philadelphia, a city in Asia Minor, Jesus says, "Because you have kept my word of patient endurance, I will keep you from the hour of trial [peirasmou] that is coming on the whole world to test the inhabitants of the earth." The time of trial in this verse is a cosmic and catastrophic one. Much of the rest of Revelation, from chapter 4 to chapter 20, plays out this time of trial. The book's author uses the strange, obscure imagery of a literary genre known as *apocalyptic* to describe this time of testing. In Mark 13 and its parallels we find a similar description of a cataclysmic time of trial that will precede the coming of a mysterious figure known as the Son of Man.

These descriptions of the cosmic time of trial have engendered much confusion and unwarranted fear throughout the history of the church. Preying on these fears has become an incredibly lucrative enterprise for a rash of self-anointed end-times experts over the past half-century or so. Unfortunately, the dangerous misinterpretations these supposed authorities propound have long since broken out of the sheltered fundamentalist enclave in which they arose and have "gone viral." The outbreak started with Hal Lindsey, whose *The Late Great Planet Earth* was the number-one bestselling nonfiction book of the entire decade of the 1970s. This end-times scenario really entered the mainstream with the publication of the *Left Behind* series of novels by Tim LaHaye and Jerry Jenkins. These books became such a phenomenon in the 1990s that many people—perhaps a majority—both inside and outside the American church now believe Lindsey's, LaHaye's, and Jenkins's interpretation to be an orthodox and long-standing part of Christian doctrine.

It is neither.

This "Rapture theology," if I may call it that, has actually been around less than two hundred years.[5] It arose as a result of a vision of Margaret MacDonald, a fifteen-year-old Scottish girl, who saw in 1830 what she described as a two-stage return of Jesus. A British evangelical preacher named Thomas Nelson Darby took MacDonald's vision and ran with it. He popularized the idea of a double return of Jesus—once to "snatch up," or rapture, his faithful ones and a second and final time to preside over the Last Judgment. The notion spread rapidly throughout both the United Kingdom and the United States.

Darby's scheme became known as "dispensationalism," because he divided human history into seven distinct periods, or dispensations, during which God governed and judged people according to different sets of rules. According to Darby, we presently live in the dispensation of the church, a period that began on the day of Pentecost and will continue until the Rapture. During this period, God deals with humankind on the basis of their response to God's offer of grace through Jesus's atoning death. The next dispensation will commence after the Rapture removes the church from the world, and will last for seven terrible years known as the Great Tribulation. In this period, all the horrors described in the book of Revelation will come to pass, including the rise of a charismatic but evil world leader known as the Beast or, in popular parlance, the Antichrist. At the end of this Tribulation, Jesus will return as a mighty warrior to utterly defeat the Beast and his forces of evil in a bloodbath called Armageddon. This great victory will usher in a millennium of bliss with Jesus reigning as king over all the earth. After that time, Satan will rebel and Jesus will defeat him and condemn him to eternal torment in a lake of fire, along with all his minions and everyone who refused to accept Jesus as his or her personal Savior. Then all the redeemed will settle in for an eternity in heaven. Everyone (except the ones treading lava in the lake of fire, of course) will live happily ever after.

That may sound rather fanciful, but only because it is. The whole scenario depends on a selective culling of texts from all over the Scriptures and their literal or loose interpretation, depending on what serves the interpreter's purposes in each instance. Nowhere in the Bible can you find this

5. For the historical information in the next several paragraphs, I am indebted to Barbara R. Rossing, *The Rapture Exposed*, 22–23.

entire scenario laid out in a coherent narrative, but this has not stopped the Darbyites from selling their system to the church and the public as gospel truth for more than a century.

The key to the continuing success of this venture was the enormous popularity of the Scofield Reference Bible. In 1909 Cyrus Scofield published a special version of the King James Bible with explanatory notes and headings based on the dispensationalists' Rapture theology. In his Bible, Scofield incorporated his interpretive notes into the biblical text itself, so that the untrained reader had a hard time distinguishing between Holy Writ and Darby's and Scofield's dubious interpretations. The Scofield Bible sold in the millions, and became a staple feature of the Fundamentalist movement in the early twentieth century and of its later offshoots, neo-fundamentalism and conservative evangelicalism. People who have grown up in these environments over the past hundred years have been steeped in dispensationalism. Add to Scofield's influence the popularity of *The Late Great Planet Earth*, the *Left Behind* novels, and the proliferation of other books, web sites, blogs, and programs on Christian TV, and one hardly wonders that such a large percentage of Christians and casual observers believe the Rapture and all the rest to be traditional and unquestionable doctrine.

When we consider the translation of the Lord's Prayer that goes, "Do not bring us into the time of trial," according to the dispensationalists' logic, we clearly see that Jesus had the Great Tribulation in view. No one in her right mind who heard the lurid and terrifying descriptions of this seven-year period would want to be around for it, so a fervent prayer for God not to bring us to that pass would be perfectly understandable. So would the second part of the petition, "Deliver us from evil."

This interpretation, however, suffers from the unfortunate problem of being an escapist fantasy that flies in the face of everything Jesus taught. In what scholars have dubbed his "little apocalypse," in the thirteenth chapter of Mark and its parallels in Matthew 24 and Luke 21, Jesus predicts a terrible future ordeal of war, siege, and destruction. Tutored by the dispensationalists, conventional wisdom makes this future event into the end of the world, but it more likely refers to the siege and destruction of Jerusalem in 69–70 CE, an event that lay forty years in Jesus's future but burned as a fresh memory from the gospel writers' past.

Regardless of the exact referent of the little apocalypse, Jesus clearly rejects the escapism of Rapture theology as an option for his disciples. In Mark 13:12–13, he warns them, "Brother will betray brother to death, and a father his child. Children will rebel against their parents and have them put to death. Everyone will hate you because of me, but *those who stand firm to the end* will be saved" (TNIV, emphasis added). This is a far cry from the Rapture enthusiasts' expectation of being snatched out of harm's way before the time of tribulation even begins. Jesus provides an assurance—"You will be saved"—but a sober one—"You must stand firm to the end." He does not offer shortcuts. Salvation comes to those who endure and remain faithful. One earns maturity through training in the school of hard knocks; it is not granted at matriculation.

When we understand peirasmos as a time of trial or testing, we begin to see the important role it plays in our spiritual development. Those who try to short-circuit the character-building process of testing resemble the people of Hadleyburg. They thought they could preserve their purity by eliminating all sources of temptation; instead, they set themselves up for a terrific fall. But if times of trial hold such positive benefits for our character and advancement as disciples, we again face that pesky question: why does Jesus tell us to pray that God would *not* lead us into them? Oughtn't we rather change our prayer as the Hadleyburgers changed their town motto— "Lead us *into* temptation"? Before we address this question, we may find it helpful to consider a second scriptural example of the use of peirasmos: Jesus's time of testing or temptation in the wilderness.

QUOTING DEUTERONOMY TO THE DEVIL[6]

Jesus experiences a time of testing in all three synoptic gospels. Matthew and Luke both take Mark's cursory account and elaborate on it in ways that suit their particular theological purposes. In each of the gospels, the testing or temptation comes on the heels of Jesus's baptism, an event that serves as the scene for one of the two heavenly declarations to or about Jesus in the gospels (the other is the transfiguration). Matthew describes the announcement this way: "As soon as Jesus was baptized, he went up out of the water. At that moment heaven was opened, and he saw the Spirit of God descending like a dove and alighting on him. And a voice from heaven said, 'This is my Son, the Beloved, with whom I am well pleased'" (Matt 3:16–17). The significance of this declaration will become clear when we examine the content of Jesus's trials/temptations.

6. A song co-written by Rich Mullins and Beaker provides the title of this section. See Mullins, "Quoting Deuteronomy to the Devil."

First, however, we should take note of how Matthew sets the stage. Immediately after the heavenly announcement, he writes, "Then Jesus was led up by the Spirit into the wilderness to be tempted by the devil" (Matt 4:1). This verse appears to contradict the wording of the Lord's Prayer, where we ask God *not* to lead us into temptation. It seems to contradict even more directly James's assertion from later in the New Testament: "No one, when tempted, should say, 'I am being tempted by God'; for God cannot be tempted by evil and he himself tempts no one" (Jas 1:13). So does God lead Jesus into temptation, or does God simply lead him into the wilderness, knowing that he will be tempted there—and does it make a difference?

I think the distinction does matter. God does not do the actual tempting, but God *does* lead Jesus into a situation in which he will be tempted. God knows that such testing has positive value. James again: "My brothers and sisters, whenever you face trials of any kind, consider it nothing but joy, because you know that the testing of your faith produces endurance; and let endurance have its full effect, so that you may be mature and complete, lacking in nothing" (Jas 1:2–4). The people of Hadleyburg would have done well to heed this advice.

After the Spirit leads him into the wilderness, Jesus fasts for forty days and forty nights, at the end of which time, Matthew tells us helpfully, "He was hungry" (Matt 4:2 TNIV). The tempter sees his chance, and says, "If you are the Son of God, command these stones to become loaves of bread" (Matt 4:3). We can almost hear the subtle inflection on the word *if*. Just before coming to the desert, Jesus heard (or *thought* he heard) the voice of God saying, "You are my Son, whom I love." But after more than a month alone in the barren and spooky hills above the Jordan valley, the sense of assurance he felt at that moment has begun to fade. The idea of turning some of these stones into bread—they look a little like loaves of bread anyway, come to think of it—starts to sound pretty good when you haven't eaten in forty days. Besides, didn't the voice say that God was well pleased with him? That gives a sort of green light, doesn't it?

But something keeps gnawing at the back of Jesus's mind that makes him hesitate. Finally, after a protracted inner struggle, Jesus finds in his memory a line from Deuteronomy: "One does not live by bread alone, but by every word that comes from the mouth of God" (Matt 4:4, citing Deut 8:3). To use the power at his command by virtue of his relationship with God to meet a personal need would be a misuse of that power.

If we go a little deeper, though, we see that this may be more than simply a personal temptation. The tempter may be suggesting that Jesus use his power as the Son of God to turn stones into bread to feed the multitudes. Where could he find a nobler or more righteous use of his power than to feed the hungry? I imagine this element of the temptation, more than the desire to assuage his own hunger, gives Jesus serious pause.

But he rejects the temptation, because he knows that the kingdom of God does not come miraculously. Mysteriously, yes, but not miraculously. I believe Jesus perceived his role to be a community-builder. He sought to revitalize and renew the people's covenant with God by creating a community of interdependence, justice, and active grace. He envisioned a countercultural community that welcomed all, but rejected the accretions of tradition that had built up on the covenant over the years and that served to alienate people from God's grace rather than inviting them to experience it. Jesus's kingdom community exercised radical equality. It embodied nonviolent resistance to the forces of empire and creative noncooperation with evil. Such a community does not spring up overnight; it must be nurtured, protected, watered, and pruned.

Consider the twelve disciples. They were awfully slow on the uptake, and showed again and again that they just didn't get Jesus's mission. He had to exercise a lot of patience to bring them along to an adequate level of understanding—and they lived and traveled with him every day! What a painstaking process Jesus must have engaged in with those who did not enjoy that privilege of proximity. The kind of community Jesus sought to build could not come as a result of a miracle, because miracles would short-circuit the process.

In the temptation scene, Jesus concludes that to perform miracles either for his own benefit or to help a large number of people in the short term would be an abuse of his power that would ultimately prove counterproductive. Miraculous shortcuts pave the way for more shortcuts, a cycle that will never produce maturity or community, and will actually harm the people the miracle worker means to help.

In the second trial that Matthew relates, the devil again introduces the subject by saying, "*If* you are the Son of God." This time the scene has shifted from the wilderness to the pinnacle of the Temple in Jerusalem. The tempter suggests to Jesus that he could throw himself from that high and prominent spot, and now he himself quotes Scripture: "For it is written," he says,

"He will command his angels concerning you
    to guard you in all your ways.
On their hands they will bear you up,
    so that you will not dash your foot against a stone" (Ps 91:11–12).

The psalmist originally addressed these lines to the nation of Israel, assuring them of God's providential care for them if they remained faithful to the covenant. Here the devil interprets the psalm messianically, with Jesus as the Son of God in the place of Israel, which the Old Testament refers to a number of times as God's "firstborn son."[7] The devil chooses this setting because the Temple serves as the center of not only religious life, but also social, economic, and political life for the Jewish descendants of Israel. The pinnacle of the Temple is the highest and most visible part of that enormous complex. If Jesus wants to declare his identity as God's Son and God's chosen instrument for the renewal of Israel and the salvation of the world, what better place could he pick to do it? The tempter here tries to entice Jesus to use spectacle and miracle to advance his cause. He rejects this temptation for the same reasons he rejected the first one.

In addition to those reasons, Jesus in this instance introduces another intriguing idea, which we see in the biblical text—again from Deuteronomy—he uses to refute the tempter. He says, "Again it is written, 'Do not put the Lord your God to the test'" (Matt 4:7, citing Deut 6:16). To take a swan dive into the crowded Temple courts, in the hope that God would send angels to catch him, would not only test God, but, ironically enough, indicate a lack of faith in God. If Jesus believed his mission was to build a kingdom community, to try to conjure one through publicity stunts and magic tricks would represent a betrayal.

Note also that the phrase "put [God] to the test" comes from the same root, peirasmos, as the temptations or trials Jesus endures here and that he instructs his disciples to pray that God would not lead them into in the Prayer. It's an interesting idea: whether or not to put God to the test *is* the test. Jesus passes.

In the third trial or temptation Jesus faces in Matthew 4, the devil makes his power play. He stops being subtle or cajoling; this time he puts all his chips in the pot and lays his cards on the table. He takes Jesus to the top of a high mountain, displays before him a panorama of "all the kingdoms of the world and their splendor" (Matt 4:8), and says quite baldly, "All these I will give you, if you will fall down and worship me" (Matt 4:9).

7. See, for example, Exodus 4:22 and Jeremiah 31:9.

As we saw in Chapter 3, Jesus does not dispute the devil's claim to be able to follow through on this promise. He gives no indication that he has seen through a lie, either. The tempter makes an offer, and Jesus takes it at face value. The kingdoms of the world and their splendor belong to the devil, and are at his disposal to give to whomever he chooses.

Jesus doesn't take the bait. In fact, he issues his most forceful rebuke yet: "Away with you, Satan! for it is written, 'Worship the Lord your God, and serve only him'" (Matt 4:10, citing Deut 6:13). He identifies the source of the temptation finally as Satan, the Adversary, and tells him—commands him, really—to get out of Dodge. Clearly, something about this particular temptation has flipped the switch in Jesus's mind so that he can recognize the tempter for who he is and reject the temptation decisively.

So far, I have been taking the temptation narrative at face value as Matthew presents it. But for most of us, the temptations or tests we undergo do not present themselves in as clear-cut a manner as these do, and our struggles with them do not resemble a conversation with an identifiable personification of temptation. We endure internal debates of long duration, often muddled and confused, which may not even strike us at first as temptations at all. I believe Jesus's experience was similar to ours. Matthew, being a good storyteller, presents them in a neat three-part narrative. But if the Incarnation is true and Jesus was a real human being with real human emotions, motivations, and vulnerabilities, we can be confident in presuming that his time of trial in the wilderness did not happen this neatly.

As Jesus struggles his way through the first two temptations, I imagine a slow realization growing in his mind, like a Polaroid photograph developing. He begins to perceive where following the easier path the tempter offers him would ultimately lead. Say he did choose to go the miracle route to feed the people and gain their favor, or the spectacle route to save the whole nation and strike fear in the hearts of their oppressors. How would that turn out? He could ride the wave of public acclaim all the way to a throne. With the power at his disposal, he could fulfill the expectations for a messiah in the mold of David, the warrior king. He could rout the Romans and set himself up in their place, ruling the world not from the seven hills of Rome but from Mount Zion in Jerusalem. If he were to go this way, the sky would be the limit. All the kingdoms of the world, and all their splendor, would be within his grasp.

That's when it dawns on him: the fantasy his fevered mind just spun, as plausible and attainable as it might be, will not lead him down the path the true Son of God must travel. In fact, it stands in direct opposition to what he has to do. If he decided to follow this path, he might as well just bow down and worship Satan now and get it over with. Because Satan really does control all the kingdoms of the world. For "world," Matthew uses the word kosmos, which we have already seen to refer to the Domination System. Not the world God created, not the world that "God so loved . . . that he gave his only begotten Son" (John 3:16 KJV), but the world created in human and demonic partnership through destructive power-over rather than life-giving power-with.

In the end, that's what tips the scale for Jesus. It makes it possible for him to say, "Away from me, Satan!" and choose his difficult path rather than the tempter's easy one. That's how he manages to forgo the world's crowns of gold and instead choose a road that will lead him to a crown of thorns. He realizes that choosing to rule the Domination System would play right into the hands of the evil one, so he commits himself to worshiping God and serving God only, no matter where it may lead.

EXPANDING THE TOOLBOX

Jesus faced temptations in the wilderness and passed the test, but that was not the end of it. Luke expresses this quite explicitly. At the conclusion of his temptation narrative, he writes, "When the devil had finished every test, he departed from [Jesus] until an opportune time" (Luke 4:13). A great number of opportune times undoubtedly arose over the course of the next months and years, but surely the most trying time for Jesus came during the events leading up to his crucifixion. I want to focus specifically upon his experience in Gethsemane because it has bearing on our interpretation of the temptation petition in the Lord's Prayer.

Mark's gospel offers the most stark and harrowing account of Jesus's agony in Gethsemane. In his portrayal, we see a frail human being in a very real struggle about how to proceed. You don't get the sense in reading Mark that Jesus views his choice to go to the cross as a foregone conclusion. For Jesus, at least, the issue remains very much in doubt almost to the last moment.

When Jesus arrives at Gethsemane, Mark tells us, "He took with him Peter and James and John, and began to be distressed and agitated. And he said to them, 'I am deeply grieved, even to death; remain here, and keep awake'" (Mark 14:33–34). After going a bit farther on his own, he practically hurls himself on the ground and prays "that, if it were possible, the hour might pass from him" (Mark 14:35). Mark does not paint a portrait of a divine being who knows the outcome of events ahead of time and can therefore face them with equanimity. Nor is this Socrates, calmly accepting the cup of hemlock and philosophically taking a sip. This is a man terror-stricken, who sees what approaches and wants to find any possible way to avoid it. This is a man in agony.

Mark tells us the content of his prayer: "Abba, Father, for you all things are possible; remove this cup from me" (Mark 14:36). Then I imagine a very long pause, during which Jesus goes through an intense inner struggle, before he utters the next line, as though it were wrenched from his lips: "Yet, not what I want, but what you want" (Mark 14:36).

Many interpret his surrender to God's will to mean that God planned Jesus's death from the beginning, which would reinforce the supposition that his primary purpose, if not his *sole* purpose, was to die for our sins. But there is another and I think much better way to interpret this prayer, and it has to do with the next part of the scene in Gethsemane. Jesus returns to where he left Peter, James, and John, only to find them sleeping. Exhausted by his struggle, he can muster only a mild rebuke: "Simon, are you asleep? Could you not keep awake one hour? Keep awake and pray that you may not come into the time of trial; the spirit indeed is willing, but the flesh is weak" (Mark 14:37–38). A mild rebuke indeed, and he offers it in compassionate tones, but his counsel here is of the gravest importance, because here again we encounter that crucial word peirasmos. Some translators use the word "temptation," while others go with "time of trial," but the idea is the same: peril awaits the disciples. A test is coming, and if they do not prepare themselves in advance, they will fail. But what kind of test?

We have come to the crux of the matter. We have here the key to our interpretation of the temptation petition of the Lord's Prayer. Citing, among other passages, the Gethsemane narratives of all three synoptic gospels, John Dominic Crossan suggests that Jesus has in mind something very specific when he tells the disciples to pray, "Lead us not into temptation, but deliver us from evil." Rather than a generic trial ("which car to buy") or temptation ("that extra dessert"), Jesus warns them against yielding to the specific temptation to use violence.[8]

To the group huddled there in Gethsemane, the warning has an immediate context: before the night is over both Jesus and his disciples will

---

8. Crossan, *The Greatest Prayer*, 167–81.

be faced with the threat of violence, and the choice of whether or not to respond in kind. But I believe we can extrapolate the temptation beyond the narrow confines of the Gethsemane story. When Jesus says, "Put your sword back into its place; for all who take the sword will perish by the sword" (Matt 26:52), he offers a maxim that holds true in every situation in every age. Once one chooses violence, even for supposedly noble purposes, one sets in motion an ever-escalating cycle of violence in which there can be no winners except the forces of evil themselves. As Simone Weil put it, "However just the cause of the conqueror may be, however just that of the conquered, the evil caused, whether by victory or by defeat, is none the less inevitable."[9]

In the collection of sayings that scholars have named Q and dated to the sixth decade of the first century CE, Jesus sends the twelve apostles out into the surrounding communities to preach the gospel, cast out demons, and heal the sick. In his instructions to them before they depart on their mission, he tells them not to take a staff (Matt 10:10). Crossan points out that a staff represented the bare minimum of protection a traveler in those days could take to defend himself against thieves, wild animals, and dogs. In this earliest and most radical version of these instructions, Jesus forbids his disciples to use violence at all, even to defend themselves. Mark's account of the instructions softens the tone by allowing them to take a staff, but we see the blanket condemnation of violence from Matthew confirmed by Jesus's words and actions at the time of his arrest.[10]

The communities of Jesus's followers regularly faced threats of violence and the temptation to employ counter-violence, both during Jesus's own lifetime and in the decades and centuries after his death and resurrection. Because the Lord's Prayer is a communal prayer, it follows that the petition about temptation involves the entire community, not just isolated individuals. Those who have committed themselves to the way of Jesus pray *together* for deliverance from the temptation to use violence. As the Gethsemane story illustrates, the means for overcoming that temptation comes through prayer and vigilance. The community that prays together and creates covenants of nonviolence among its members has a much better chance of resisting the urge to take up arms in the heat of the moment.

9. Weil, *Notebooks*, 25. Citation is to the 2004 edition.

10. Crossan, *The Greatest Prayer*, 179–80. Crossan explains that the version of the instructions in Matthew predates the one in Mark, even though Mark was written first, because Matthew's version comes from the Q source, which scholars date to the 50s, around twenty years before Mark.

Christian communities and individuals that sleep, metaphorically speaking, when they should be wrestling with this temptation in prayer are far more likely to give in to violence when the chips are down.

I believe Jesus proposed to renew the covenant between the people and God by creating an egalitarian, cooperative, and countercultural community as an alternative to the Domination System. If so, then the notion that he was talking about the temptation to resort to violence becomes more plausible. Think back to the third temptation in Matthew 4, when Jesus came to the realization that to "gain the whole world" would cause him to "forfeit [his] soul," as he puts it in another part of the gospel.[11] He saw that to achieve glory and power in the Domination System would mean to bow down and worship the devil.

More than that, if he gave in to the temptation to use violence *in God's name* or to advance God's purposes, he would take God's hallowed name in vain (see Chapter 2). This provides the clue we need to understand why Jesus tells us to pray that God would not lead us into temptation. To give in to the temptation of violence is one thing, but to baptize our violence by claiming to wield it in the name of God—as though God *led* us to that particular choice—has much more serious implications. I don't believe I overstate the case when I put a name to that form of rationalization: *blasphemy*.

But then, we live in a blasphemous age. Too many of us seem not only willing but *eager* to call on God to bless our acts of violence. One can find extremists in all of the world's major religions who believe they have a divine mandate to wage holy war against the infidels. Many born-again Christians supported the US's invasion of Iraq, and some high-profile Christian leaders have even called for agents of our government to carry out political assassinations.[12] By and large, US Christians accept the notion of "American exceptionalism," which claims a special relationship between God and our country. In our belligerent national pride we insist that *our* violence, *our* wars, *our* blatant use of power-over are righteous acts performed for noble purposes. God, or rather America's version of God, smiles on us when we go to war.

But America's God and the God whom Jesus called *Abba* are two different deities. Jesus receives ultimate confirmation of the nonviolent nature

11. See Mark 8:36 and parallels.

12. For example, in 2005, Pat Robertson, founder of the Christian Broadcasting Network, suggested on his TV program, *The 700 Club*, that covert operatives should "take out" Venezuelan president Hugo Chavez. See Goodstein, "Robertson." He later apologized for the remark but did not disavow the principle of diplomacy by assassination.

of God during his struggle in Gethsemane. It's not as though he doesn't have options. As he himself says when the Temple police come to arrest him and a disciple draws his sword and wounds one of them, "Do you think that I cannot appeal to my Father, and he will at once send me more than twelve legions of angels [to fight on my behalf]?" (Matt 26:53). If he had jumped from the pinnacle of the Temple during his time of testing in the desert, God would undoubtedly have sent an angel to catch him, and if he called for them now, the angel armies would come to fight for him. But either choice would spell defeat. Jesus came to challenge, undermine, and ultimately dismantle the Domination System—something he cannot do using that System's weapons.

We have yet to learn this lesson, and we continue to resist it, even in Christian circles. In the US at least, Christian pacifists are few and far between. Most Christians I know will tolerate some degree of violence, from the minimal and most easily justified level of defending oneself and one's family to the extreme of waging aggressive war. A great many Christians accuse those who disavow the use of violence in any form as naive and unrealistic. But Jesus rejects violence, even violence used in his defense. He rebukes the disciple who tries to defend him, saying, "Put your sword back into its place; for all who take the sword will perish by the sword" (Matt 26:52). He goes through an agonizing struggle in Gethsemane—Luke describes an anguish so severe that his sweat turns to blood—but at the end of it he musters the strength to say, "Not what I want, but what you want," and stick to it.

One cannot say the same of the disciples. They sleep while he wrestles in prayer, so they are not prepared when the chips are down. Earlier that evening, Jesus predicted they would desert him, and they all objected, pounding their chests and saying, "Never!" Peter went so far as to say he would lay down his own life rather than abandon Jesus. But then three times Jesus finds him sleeping when he should be praying. Is it any surprise that, after Jesus rejects the disciples' feeble attempt at violent defense, Peter takes to his heels with all the others, leaving Jesus to his fate?

An old saying goes, "If your only tool is a hammer, all problems look like nails." The disciples' failure at the scene of Jesus's arrest should serve to instruct us. Many Christians justify their support for violence by saying they believe in just war theory. One of the criteria of that theory, however, stipulates that violence be used only as a last resort, after all other options have been exhausted. But for us, like for the disciples, violence often seems the first and only resort. The disciples lash out immediately with the sword, and when Jesus rebukes them for it, they don't know what else to do, so they run away. We should try to learn from their failure and expand our own toolboxes. A good collection contains many other useful tools besides swords and hammers.

Fortunately, we have many examples to follow of persons with ex-panded toolboxes. The historic "peace churches" of the Anabaptist tradi-tion—the Mennonites, Amish, Quakers, and others—have long stood staunchly on the side of pacifism. By modeling negotiation, listening, and forgiveness instead of combativeness, they show a way to resolve conflicts without violence. Groups such as Human Rights Watch and Amnesty International use public pressure, not arms, to convince oppressive gov-ernments to release political prisoners and end human rights abuses. The Truth and Reconciliation hearings spearheaded by Desmond Tutu helped South Africans deal with the scars of apartheid without descending into a bloodbath of retaliatory violence. John P. Burgess has demonstrated the vi-tal role the church played in both providing a theological framework for the democracy movement in East Germany in the 1980s and creating a space for that movement to germinate, which ultimately led to a bloodless revolu-tion, the fall of the Berlin Wall, and the end of the communist regime.[13] Churches, synagogues, people of faith from other religious traditions, and conscientious nonbelievers used nonviolent resistance to advance the civil rights, anti-war, anti-nuclear, and other movements in recent American history. And the Interfaith Alliance and similar groups model cooperation and dialogue between adherents of different traditions, offering a sorely needed alternative to the suspicion, misunderstanding, and violence that characterizes so much of the intersection of religions in our world.

We also need to learn from Jesus's successful resistance to temptation in the wilderness and again in Gethsemane. When he equated participation in the Domination System with worship of the devil, he realized a profound truth. The Domination System thrives on violence, coercion, and—well, domination. Those elements, known collectively as power-over, form part of the System's foundation, without which it could not long survive. By refusing to play by the System's rules or to use its tools, Jesus dealt it a griev-ous blow.

Perhaps the best presentation of these ideas in the realm of literature can be found in the work of J.R.R. Tolkien. In his master work, *The Lord*

---

13. Burgess, *East German Church*.

of the Rings, he depicts the Dark Lord Sauron as having amassed his great armies and built his mighty fortress of Barad-dûr with the help of the One Ring. When he first forged the Ring, he invested it with a great part of his own power, cruelty, and menace, so in a very real way the Ring shares the character of its maker. That explains why anyone who tries to use the Ring for his own ends, even ends we would call good, will ultimately fail. The Ring will corrupt him so that in the end he resembles Sauron himself. No one can resist the Ring for long; it will ultimately destroy anyone who tries to use it.[14]

We can say the same of violence and power-over. They infect everything they touch and stain all who try to use them, even for good purposes. Martin Luther King Jr. joined a long line of wise prophets when he said, "Returning hate for hate multiplies hate, adding deeper darkness to a night already devoid of stars. Darkness cannot drive out darkness; only light can do that. Hate cannot drive out hate; only love can do that. Hate multiplies hate [and] violence multiplies violence . . . in a descending spiral of destruction."[15]

We find the temptation to employ the weapons of the Domination System for good, even for God, powerfully seductive. But it is a trap. When you play by the devil's rules, using the devil's tools, it doesn't matter which side you *think* you are on. The devil always wins. We have seen this scenario played out over and over again throughout world history. Vendettas and clan feuds repay blood with blood in a never-ending cycle. Misplaced religious zeal sparks *jihad* and Crusades, suicide bombings and drone strikes. The ideological contest known as the Cold War embroils countries such as Nicaragua, Angola, and Vietnam in devastating "hot" wars and starts an arms race that still haunts us with the possibility of global obliteration. All the way to today, when the Israelis and Palestinians who occupy the same small stretch of real estate can't find a way to live together, but rather choose reprisals over negotiation and escalation of conflict over peace.

There is good news, though. There is hope. Remember how Sauron founded Barad-dûr with the power of the Ring? Frodo Baggins, one of the smallest, weakest, and seemingly most insignificant of creatures, opts not to wield the Ring but instead to carry it to Mordor to cast it into the flames where it was forged. In doing this he subverts the rules and expectations of the Domination System, causing Barad-dûr to crumble and breaking the

14. See Tolkien, *Lord of the Rings,* 46–7, 267.

15. King Jr., *Strength to Love,* 53.

power of the Dark Lord. Of course, Frodo does not find it easy, and loses a part of himself in the struggle (literally, since he needs the "help" of Gollum, who bites off Frodo's ring finger before falling into the Cracks of Doom with his prize). But he does it. His efforts and motives are so unexpected, so counter to Sauron's way of thinking, that the forces of evil have no defense against Frodo's mission. Sauron's vulnerability lies in his conviction that he is invulnerable, and that leads to his undoing.[16]

Recent history also gives us reasons to hope. Gandhi chooses *satyagraha* ("truth force") over armed force and overthrows British rule in India without violence. Tutu and Mandela choose reconciliation over revenge and lead South Africa out of the age of apartheid with far less bloodshed than expected. King and Parks and Abernathy meet hate with love and conquer the violence of segregation through stubborn but peaceful resistance. And groups and individuals all over the world have bonded together to raise their voices and exercise "people power" to ban land mines, end wars, dismantle nuclear weapons, stop the spread of deadly diseases, abolish the death penalty, and more.

Jesus, of course, serves as the paradigm for all these efforts. His victory over temptation, his choice to absorb the evil and violence directed at him and respond with love, has made it possible for others—for us—to achieve the same victory. By rejecting all the hammers available to him in the devil's toolbox, Jesus is able to subvert the Domination System, catch it unawares, and deal it the fatal blow from which springs hope and salvation for the world.

The work is not yet finished, of course. The blow to the Domination System was fatal, but not immediately so. It lumbers on, and its power often seems to grow rather than diminish. We must therefore join Jesus in subversive, nonviolent resistance to all the forces and seductions of the System. Every time we yield to the temptation to use violence, we play by the System's rules and allow it to continue. Every time we resist that temptation—especially the temptation to do it in the name of God—we shake the foundations of the fortress. We remind the powers of evil that their

---

16. Gandalf explains the logic behind the "foolish" course of seeking to destroy the Ring in the Council of Elrond: "Well, let folly be our cloak, a veil before the eyes of the Enemy! For he is very wise, and weighs all things to a nicety in the scales of his malice. But the only measure that he knows is desire, desire for power; and so he judges all hearts. Into his heart the thought will not enter that any will refuse it, that having the Ring we may seek to destroy it. If we seek this, we shall put him out of reckoning" (Tolkien, *Lord of the Rings*, 269).

destruction is assured. And we claim one more piece of ground for the kingdom of God.

To do these things, however, we need to be prepared and disciplined. We must wrestle in prayer with our own violent tendencies and the temptation to become complicit with the Domination System. More than that, we must keep on the lookout for other tools to add to our toolboxes—creative tools we can use to build a more just, peaceful world. Jesus must not find us sleeping when we should be praying. So let us pray and keep on praying, "Lead us not into temptation, but deliver us from evil."

7

All's Right with the World

*For thine is the kingdom and the power
and the glory forever.*

IN "PIPPA'S SONG," ROBERT Browning writes:

> God's in His heaven—
> All's right with the world![1]

Even a cursory look at the state of our world, however, debunks the notion that all is right with it. Fortunately for us, we can assert not only that God is in heaven, but also that God *aren't* in heaven. The classical Christian doctrine of the Incarnation asserts that God has left the heaven ghetto and, in the person of Jesus and through the continuing work of the Holy Spirit, has cast God's lot with humanity and the rest of creation. We do not worship or serve the Deists' clockmaker God, but rather a passionate God up to the elbows in this messy, troubled world, suffering with those who suffer, mourning with those who mourn, and rejoicing with those who rejoice. God has never been content to lounge in a hammock. The very hope of the world rests in the truth that God is not sequestered in heaven.

But one must acknowledge that all is *not* right with the world. The greed, violence, injustice, and barbarism of the Domination System still

1. Browning, "Pippa's Song," n.p.

hold sway in many nations, corporations, families, neighborhoods, houses of worship, and individual human hearts. Around the world people die of hunger, die in wars, die from drone strikes, die from preventable illnesses. As I write this, turmoil and violence rage in Syria, Ukraine, the Central African Republic, and Iraq. Religious extremism and persecution make life miserable for people in Iran, Iraq, Pakistan, Nigeria, Eritrea, and Sri Lanka; tyrants hold sway in North Korea, Uzbekistan, and Zimbabwe; and gender and sexual minorities face grave risks in Uganda, Russia, and Jamaica. In the United States, the divide between the rich and the poor continues to grow; the public education system in many cities and towns is in shambles; a major American city has declared bankruptcy; more than two million people—most of them black, brown, and poor—populate the nation's prisons; racial injustice and inequity continue virtually unabated; and Washington grinds ever more deeply into ideological gridlock.

All is definitely not right with the world.

Yet even in the midst of all these seemingly insoluble problems and intractable conflicts, hope abides. This hope finds its basis in the mission of Jesus of Nazareth, now carried on by the church and others of goodwill through the empowerment and guidance of the Holy Spirit. Bread for the World, for example, uses the combined influence of tens of thousands of US citizens to bring about government policies that fight hunger and poverty in this country and around the world. Christian Peacemaker Teams equip volunteers in the principles of nonviolence and conflict resolution and send them into conflict zones to assist local groups seeking to confront systems of oppression and violence. World Vision personnel work in over a hundred countries to provide emergency relief and long-term development assistance to tackle the root causes of poverty, hunger, and injustice. The Reformation Project trains LGBT Christians and straight allies to take the gospel of inclusion to their local churches with the goal of affirming and including LGBT persons in all aspects of church life. When we look around, we do see reasons for hope.

Next to the enormity of the world's problems, it may seem a fragile hope, and often a flickering one. In *The Lord of the Rings*, Gandalf says of Frodo's mission to destroy the Ring, "There never was much hope. . . . Just a fool's hope."[2] Our hope in the final victory of the kingdom of God often feels like a fool's hope, but it hangs on tenaciously nevertheless.

2. Tolkien, *Lord of the Rings*, 815.

The Lord's Prayer ends on this note of hopefulness. Week after week, Christians the world over voice this foolish yet persistent hope when we pray, "For thine is the kingdom and the power and the glory forever."

THE ODYSSEY OF THEODICY

This concluding doxology is the only part of the Lord's Prayer as we have it today, besides "amen," that appears in neither Matthew nor Luke. For this reason, most Roman Catholic and Eastern Orthodox liturgies do not include it as part of the prayer. It first appeared in the *Didache*, a church manual of sorts from the late first or early second century, whose name means the "Teaching of the Twelve Apostles." But Jewish prayers at the time commonly included doxologies, so the Evangelists probably assumed one would be added by the congregation saying the Prayer as a matter of course.[3] Some interpreters have even suggested that the rather abrupt endings of both Matthew's and Luke's versions of the Prayer indicate that they expected free petitions *and* a concluding doxology to come after the formal part of the prayer.[4]

Whatever the case, this doxology has come down to us as an integral part of the Lord's Prayer from the earliest decades of the church. Countless Christians recite or sing it Sunday after Sunday without giving a thought to its origin. It is simply part of the Prayer (or, in the case of Roman Catholics, the Eucharistic liturgy), and for many the most stirring part.

It stirs us because it introduces that element of hope that stands in defiance to all the dysfunction and evil in the world that we saw above. In spite of the multifarious and plausible grounds for hopelessness, the doxology declares that evil will not have the last word. In the end, love will win. God's kingdom will come in its fullness, and God will overcome all that stands opposed to God's designs. In the midst of the brokenness of the world, in the midst of evil, in the midst of the Domination System and our participation in it, we say, "Thine is the kingdom and the power and the glory forever." No wonder the liturgy of the Eucharist in the Episcopal Book of Common Prayer has the priest say, in introducing the people's recitation of the Lord's Prayer, "And now, as our Savior Christ has taught us, we are *bold* to say. . . ."[5] It is indeed a bold declaration of faith and hope.

3. Ayo, *The Lord's Prayer*, 197–8.
4. See, for instance, Bruner, *Christbook*, 315.
5. The Episcopal Church, "Holy Eucharist, Rite II," 369 (emphasis added).

But not, ultimately, a foolhardy one. We do not engage in mere wishful thinking when we pray this doxology. The life, death, and resurrection of Jesus Christ form the basis for this hope, and the gift of the Spirit seals and guarantees the fulfillment of the promises announced in that "Christ event." Promises such as these:

> Then people will come from east and west, from north and south, and will eat in the kingdom of God. Indeed, some are last who will be first, and some are first who will be last (Luke 13:29–30).

> I am convinced that neither death, nor life, nor angels, nor rulers, nor things present, nor things to come, nor powers, nor height, nor depth, nor anything else in all creation, will be able to separate us from the love of God in Christ Jesus our Lord (Rom 8:38–39).

> The creation itself will be set free from its bondage to decay and will obtain the freedom of the glory of the children of God (Rom 8:21).

> Then I saw a new heaven and a new earth. . . . And I saw the holy city, the New Jerusalem, coming down out of heaven from God, prepared as a bride adorned for her husband. And I heard a loud voice from the throne saying, "See, the home of God is among mortals. He will dwell with them as their God; they will be his people, and God himself will be with them; he will wipe every tear from their eyes. Death will be no more; mourning and crying and pain will be no more, for the first things have passed away." And the one who was seated on the throne said, "See, I am making all things new" (Rev 21:1–5).

> We know that the one who raised the Lord Jesus will raise us also with Jesus, and will bring us with you into his presence (2 Cor 4:14).

> When we cry, "Abba! Father!" it is [the Spirit of God] bearing witness with our spirit that we are children of God, and if children, then heirs, heirs of God and joint heirs with Christ—if, in fact, we suffer with him so that we may also be glorified with him. I consider that the sufferings of this present time are not worth comparing with the glory about to be revealed in us (Rom 8:15–18).

. . . and many more besides. We have considerable basis for hope.

What accounts for the stark divergence between these promises and the deplorable state of world affairs? People have advanced a lot of theories over the centuries to explain this, many of them falling under the heading of *theodicy*, or the defense of God's goodness in light of the reality of evil. Strident atheism has been making a comeback in recent years, and one of the strongest arguments against the existence of a loving God is the persistence of evil in the world. Many Christian thinkers have realized this—perhaps because, like me (and maybe like you as well), they have recognized the plausibility of the atheists' arguments—and have embarked on various forms of theodicy in search of credible responses to them.

The essential challenge of theodicy is to try to reconcile three apparently irreconcilable axioms:

- God is completely good and loving;

- God is completely powerful; and

- Evil persists in the world God created.

How is it possible, theodicy asks, for all three to be true?

The most common answer comes back that all three are *not* true. Some thinkers have denied the reality of evil, calling it an illusion or merely a matter of perspective: what from our limited point of view appears evil may look entirely different from God's eternal and universal perspective. Or what we call evil may really just be character-building material, like the times of trial we encountered in the last chapter—God allows us to experience what we think of as evil in order to grow us into mature and self-actualized beings.

Others reject the idea of God's goodness. Evil is real and God's power is real, but we're not dealing with a benevolent God. Rather, we have a supremely powerful Being who either doesn't care about our suffering or actively seeks our destruction. In either case, this betrays a pretty bleak view of the universe, and many people have latched onto it as a reason to reject God entirely or as a justification for their own self-centered, uncharitable, and destructive attitudes and behaviors.

Still others affirm the reality of evil and the goodness of God, but question God's power. A common form of this argument holds that God's deep love for humanity, coupled with God's utter commitment to maintaining human freedom, leads God to impose strict self-limitations so as not to abrogate our freewill. We make free choices that God knows will be harmful to us and to others, but because of God's prior commitment to nonintervention, God allows those decisions to go forward.

A more sophisticated version of this argument comes from what is known as process theology. Taking as their starting point the accounts of creation in Genesis 1 and 2, in which God does not create *ex nihilo* (out of nothing), but rather seeks to impose order on pre-existing chaos, process thinkers suggest that the struggle to bring order has never ceased for God. Something about the created universe remains essentially chaotic and perpetually resistant to God's efforts to direct it in an orderly or positive direction. It's entropy on a cosmic scale. In a sense, the universe is self-destructive, so it should come as no surprise that we have self-destructive (and other-destructive) tendencies as well.

In the process scenario, God's power is limited. One can rightly call God the Supreme Being, a marvelously powerful entity or force, but not an infinitely powerful one. As a result, God cannot coerce the creation to go the way God wants it to go. God must use the power of persuasion rather than coercion, and we get a picture of God locked in a constant struggle with recalcitrant matter, seeking in God's great love to persuade a rebellious creation to follow a course that would be better for all involved.

Some theologians have created a fourth option (although others see it as merely an offshoot or subset of process theology). They do not limit God's power, but say it takes a different form from how we ordinarily conceive of power. When we think of power, we almost automatically define it in terms of coercive, *brute* power—what feminist theologians call (and in this book I have been calling) power-over. This sort of power gets things done and doesn't care how anyone else feels about it. Our culture celebrates this kind of power in the military, in the sports world, and in the boardroom. This kind of power has held sway throughout the world from time immemorial. The strong over the weak. The rich over the poor. Men over women. Parents over children. Masters over slaves. Power-over serves as the animating force of the Domination System.

These quasi-process theologians contend that God's power should not be conceived in terms of power-over, but rather power-with. This kind of power values growth, healing, and relationships over what power-over advocates would call effectiveness. Power-with is non-hierarchical and egalitarian—it seeks to share decision-making and leadership authority. It seeks to empower the other, even if in the short run that amounts to a diminution of one's own power, because it does not view empowerment as a zero-sum game. Practitioners of power-with know that when one party freely relinquishes authority or hegemony, broad vistas of possibility open up for everyone. Jesus exercised, and his kingdom community embodied, this kind of power. What's more, power-with characterizes and defines God's relationship with the world.

You've probably already figured out which approach to theodicy I find most compelling. Not that I don't see its liabilities. Whether you describe God's power as essentially limited, self-constrained, or redefined as power-with, a non-coercive God is not particularly satisfying when one ponders great evils such as the rape of Nanking or the Rwandan genocide. When we come face to face with such atrocities, even a committed process theologian may be tempted to cry out to God, "How long, O Lord? How long before you put a stop to this?"

Which brings us back to the doxology of the Lord's Prayer. In a world such as ours, how can we possibly say, "For thine is the kingdom and the power and the glory forever," except in parody or the bitterest irony? How do we get a meaningful handle on the hope that sentence awakens in us?

ALREADY AND NOT YET

Songwriter Derek Webb has composed some brilliant, controversial, funny, and infuriating songs in his twenty-year career as a member of Caedmon's Call and as a solo artist. One of his most haunting, stark, and beautiful compositions is called "This Too Shall Be Made Right." In it he addresses deep and troubling issues without blinking or trying to soften their impact on the world and on human lives. But then he follows each of these litanies of the world's ills with this sublime refrain: "This too shall be made right."

In what I consider the most powerful verse of the song, Webb parodies the passage from the third chapter of Ecclesiastes that everyone knows from the Byrds' song "Turn! Turn! Turn!"—"To everything there is a season, and a time for every purpose under heaven" (Eccl 3:1). I have for a long time considered this passage suspect as an expression of the wisdom and goodness of God—it seems much more like the cynical philosophy of a world-weary "Preacher." It seems Webb feels the same way. He sings:

> There's a time for peace and there is a time for war,
> a time to forgive and a time to settle the score,
> a time for babies to lose their lives,
> a time for hunger and genocide,
> and this too shall be made right.[6]

---

6. Webb, "This Too Shall Be Made Right."

In another song from the same album, Webb hints that this as-yet unfulfilled day when all will be made right has already been inaugurated in the life and ministry of Jesus.[7] When we combine the sentiments from these two songs, we get a pretty good distillation of a time-honored interpretation of the meaning of the kingdom of God. As we saw above in Chapter 1, a great deal of confusion has resulted over the centuries of church history from Matthew's use of "heaven" as a circumlocution for "God." This pious choice of Matthew's unfortunately led to the misconstrual of "kingdom of heaven" as simply "heaven." This made Matthew seem to refer to an otherworldly destination instead of a profoundly this-worldly process or mission. From there it took only a short step to reach an expectation of "Kingdom Come," a realization of the kingdom of God sometime in the far future, and a functional equivalent of the end of time.

To correct this misinterpretation, biblical scholars point out that the Scriptures refer to the kingdom as both a present reality—"The kingdom of God is among you" (Luke 17:21)—and as a future hope—"Keep watch, because you do not know on what day your Lord will come" (Matt 24:42 TNIV). The New Testament and subsequent Christian theology hold the two ideas in tension in a dialectical relationship. Scholars often refer to this dialectic by the shorthand "already and not yet." The Christ event—the totality of Jesus's mission, passion, and resurrection—inaugurated the kingdom, so one can say legitimately that the kingdom has *already* come and is in operation. But one can say with equal validity that the kingdom has *not yet* arrived in its fullness. As Christians, we live in the "in-between" time when the kingdom is both now *and* not yet. We seek to recognize where the kudzu has already taken root and work to facilitate its spread. At the same time, we see how much ground still needs to be covered, and long for the day of consummation, when the vines of God's reign will have engulfed all the world.

Webb's songs point to what God calls us all to do during our brief sojourn in the world: to live faithfully in the now while continually longing for and looking forward to the not yet. The doxology of the Lord's Prayer offers us a regular reminder of both these points. "For thine *is*"—a present reality now—"the kingdom and the power and the glory *forever*"—the consummation lies in the future, but the victory has been won and God's final sovereignty will be eternal.

---

7. Webb, "A Love That's Stronger Than Our Fear."

From this perspective, the terrible state of the world's affairs takes on a whole new aspect. I would never minimize the immensity of injustice or the painful reality of suffering that people the world over go through every day. I have done some suffering of my own, so I know the pain is real and consequential. But it's a matter of degree. Paul writes to the church in Corinth, "If anyone is in Christ, there is a new creation: everything old has passed away; see, everything has become new!" (2 Cor 5:17). Note that Paul does not call *that person* a new creation; he says *there is* a new creation. The moment anyone finds life through and in Jesus Christ, the world is made anew. Death and hell and all the forces of the Domination System are powerless before this renewal. As Frederick Buechner writes in *Godric*, "All the death that ever was, set next to life, would scarcely fill a cup."[8]

THINE, NOT THEIRS

The Prayer's doxology issues not only a call to hope, but also a call to defiance. As we saw in Chapter 3, where we put the emphasis in these sentences matters. The declaration, "*Thine* is the kingdom and the power and the glory forever," at once affirms God's sovereignty and denies all other claimants to kingdom, power, or glory. In the concluding chapter I will discuss Jesus's warning to "let your word be 'Yes, yes,' or 'No, no'" (Matt 5:37), but sometimes yes and no go together. Every "yes" to God is a "no" to the powers. Every declaration of allegiance to one power necessitates the exclusion of another power that wants our allegiance for itself. Jesus also says in the Sermon on the Mount, "No one can serve two masters; for a slave will either hate the one and love the other, or be devoted to the one and despise the other" (Matt 6:24).

For Jesus's first followers, the powers vying for the kingdom and power and glory were pretty cut and dried. First, always first, was the Roman Empire. All other competitors paled in comparison. Rome itself was dubbed the Eternal City, and the Caesars had similar hopes and pretensions for their imperial rule. The early Christians, from the time of Peter and Paul in the mid-first century to the advent of Constantine in the early fourth, periodically faced official persecution by the state. One of the principal reasons was that they refused to offer the customary pinch of incense to the *genius* (the generative principle or guardian spirit) of Caesar.[9] When church

8. Buechner, *Godric*, 96.

9. Official persecution of the Jesus movement did not occur until at least twenty years

and state are one, any act of religious subversion automatically becomes a punishable political offense. Roman writers derided the Christians, calling them atheists because they did not worship the pantheon of pagan divinities, and seditionists and traitors because they would not do their civic duty by making an offering on behalf of the emperor.

In the church of my childhood, I often heard a verse from Romans quoted as an indication that it was a cinch to "get saved." Any obstacles that might exist resided within one's rebellious heart, but one could readily surmount them through a simple act of repentance. Paul writes, "If you confess with your lips that Jesus is Lord and believe in your heart that God raised him from the dead, you will be saved" (Rom 10:9). See how easy that is? Incidentally, the greater emphasis always fell on the "believe in your heart" bit. But for Paul's first-century audience, "confess with your lips" posed the bigger problem, and they found the decision to make that confession far from easy. Declaring, "Jesus is Lord," besides being ludicrous or scandalous to many who heard it, meant at the same time, "Caesar is *not* Lord," a highly seditious sentiment. The Emperor was the only Lord in town, and he countenanced no competitors. Far from being easy, saying, "Jesus is Lord," could be a matter of life and death.

The same follows for the doxology. If the kingdom and power and glory belong to God, then they do not belong to Caesar. They do not belong to the Temple. They do not belong to the church. They do not belong to America, capitalism, socialism, or any political party or ideology. They do not belong to money, sex, beauty, or even family. They do not belong to the Domination System or any of its constituent powers or minions. The kingdom, power, and glory belong to God and God alone. Forever.

---

after the death of Jesus and was sporadic, at most, until the very end of the first century. Furthermore, participation in the cult of the emperor was, at first, not mandatory. Such worship did later become, however, a strong indicator of one's allegiance to the Empire; as a result, pagan opponents used the Christians' refusal to offer the sacrifice as the grounds (or at least as a pretext) for accusing them of undermining the social order. In about 155 CE, the authorities arrested Polycarp, the Christian bishop of Smyrna, during a wave of persecution in that city. The proconsul tried to persuade him to offer the standard sacrifice to Caesar. He implored him, "'Have respect for thine age . . . swear by the genius of Caesar; repent and say, Away with the atheists. . . . Swear the oath,' urged the proconsul, 'and I will release thee; revile the Christ.' Polycarp said, 'Fourscore and six years have I been his servant, and he hath done me no wrong. How then can I blaspheme my King who saved me?'" (*Letter of Smyrnaeans*, 9:2–3.) The proconsul finally acceded to the demands of the pagan crowd and sentenced Polycarp to be burned at the stake.

Like the Roman Emperors, God brooks no competitors, either. Allegiance to God is an all-or-nothing proposition. Fortunately for us, vacillating and idolatrous as we are, God's character differs from that of the Caesars. God traffics not in coercive violence and brutality, but in forgiveness, mercy, and grace.

This doxology presents a challenge to everyone who dares utter it, but American citizens face especially great perils. In the United States, national pride and religious feeling are conflated to a bewildering degree. It started as early as the time of John Winthrop, who preached a sermon to his fellow pilgrims on the *Arbella* during their voyage to the Massachusetts Bay Colony in 1630, extolling that new society as a "city upon a hill" and an example to every other nation. It continues to the present day, when "God Bless America" sounds more like a foregone conclusion, or even a demand, than a humble plea.

Many Americans throughout our history have supposed that we have a special and preferential relationship with the Creator—so much so that a widespread sense of righteousness has managed to survive some pretty appalling behavior. Even with our history of slavery, genocide against native Americans, environmental degradation, and so on, many still consider it an article of faith that God has granted us most-favored-nation status for all time. Our national blind spot is *humongous*.

We have stirred together God and country into such a smooth batter that many American Christians find no contradiction in reciting the Lord's Prayer on Sunday and the Pledge of Allegiance on Monday. Not that there is anything inherently wrong with pledging allegiance to the flag and the country for which it stands, as long as we bear in mind that our national allegiance must always be subordinate. Saying, "Thine is the kingdom and the power and the glory forever," leaves no room for other claimants to our primary allegiance. When we pray this Prayer, we declare ourselves to be worshipers of God and disciples of Jesus before all else. We may have secondary allegiances—nation, family, church, and so on—as long as they do not conflict with our primary commitment to God and God's kingdom.

Unfortunately, we very often get it backwards. Too many times have I heard someone say, "Sure, I'm a Christian, but I'm an American first," usually in connection with some military action or international crisis. Not to put too fine a point on it, but if you identify yourself as *anything* else first, you are not a Christian. A Christian by definition says and believes, "Jesus is Lord." The first Christians gave themselves up to crucifixion or dismemberment by wild animals in the arena because of the sanctity of that confession. They were Christians first, last, and only, and they paid the price for their commitment in blood. When I consider their example, or that of the millions of Christians today who face persecution for their faith, remaining steadfast as they endure ostracism, threats, and violence, I wonder about the quality of my own confession of Jesus as Lord. When the chips are down, will my commitment to Jesus and to God's reign measure up?

THE INVITATION

The Lord's Prayer offers us an invitation. It provides an outline—a kingdom manifesto—of what Jesus wants to accomplish in the world. But he has never intended to do it on his own. At every step along the way he says to us, "Join me in this. It's the best thing you'll ever be a part of." The doxology tells us why.

Notice that we say, "*For* thine is the kingdom. . . . " "For," of course, means "because," and it refers back to the body of the Prayer. All the things we assert about God—God's holiness, compassion, and justice—and about God's kingdom—food for the hungry, release from indebtedness, rejection of the Domination System—we say *because of* what we proclaim in the doxology. Because the kingdom and the power and glory belong to God, and because God has called us into communion with God and God's Son, and because Jesus invites us to pray in this way, we are bold to say these simple yet earth-shattering words.

When we pray the doxology, we acknowledge before God the truth and sincerity in which we have offered up the foregoing, and we say that we want to be a part of God's kingdom work. We want to respond to the invitation.

Conclusion

Marching Orders

Amen.

THE LORD'S PRAYER, WHILE arguably the most universally accepted and practiced element of Christian worship, is also one of the most misunderstood. More than two billion people around the globe pray the Prayer in their corporate worship or personal devotional practices. How many of us understand the subversive, even revolutionary character of what we are praying? And if we did, how many would continue to pray it?

Routines and rituals enrich our lives. They help to ground us in a tradition larger than ourselves. They give us an unchanging standard by which to measure our progress in various ventures. They help us to understand what is important and keep us from becoming self-absorbed. Rituals in religious life—the Eucharist, baptism, daily prayers, and so on—serve all these purposes.

Unfortunately, rituals and routines have the tendency to become—you guessed it, routine. The fault, however, lies not in our rituals but in ourselves. We find it next to impossible to maintain the same level of intensity or attention when we repeat the same practices over time. It may be unfair, in fact, to call this condition we all share a problem. It's just part of human nature. Those of us who recite the Lord's Prayer regularly, either in a corporate worship setting or on our own, tend to lose the thread in this way. Many times I have found my mind wandering as I say the Prayer. My voice can speak the words without error, but my brain is occupied with any number of other things.

That is the danger of familiarity. And that is why we need to look at our rituals from a different angle from time to time. It helps us to try to hear the Prayer again for the first time, to paraphrase Marcus Borg.[1] In this book, I have tried to hold up the Lord's Prayer at an angle from which you may not have looked at it before. I hope this different perspective, whether you agree with what I have had to say or not, has enabled you to hear the Prayer afresh. I further hope that in hearing it afresh, you have recognized its continuing relevance and its compelling call to action in the world, in partnership with Jesus and our Father who aren't in heaven.

We close the Prayer by saying, "Amen." Like the doxology, this word appears in neither Matthew's nor Luke's version of the Prayer, but has become standard and accepted usage now. "Amen" means "so be it." When we say it at the conclusion of a prayer, we signal our agreement with the content of that prayer. When we say it at the close of the *Lord's* Prayer, we express our agreement with the Lord, the one who taught us to pray in the first place. Because of the Prayer's character as a manifesto of the kingdom of God, our response of "Amen" resembles a soldier's "Yes, sir," or "Yes, ma'am," after the commanding officer has given him his marching orders.

WHAT DID WE JUST AGREE TO, EXACTLY?

After considering the radical nature of the Lord's Prayer, we may feel a little like a dazed couple sitting in the office of a fast-talking car salesperson. While she has gone off to make copies of the documents they have signed, the husband turns to the wife with a dumb look on his face and says, "What did we just agree to, exactly? Did we just buy a car we can't afford?"

The Lord's Prayer is kind of like that. We're not really sure we can afford to get involved in the work of the kingdom to the degree Jesus clearly demands of us. We're not sure we are ready to commit to Jesus's social program. It all seems so . . . heavy.

So before we take a look back at what we have learned about Jesus's program as outlined in the Prayer, let us hear some good news. In Matthew 11:28–30, Jesus issues an invitation to the multitudes to become his disciples. He says, "Come to me, all you that are weary and are carrying

1. Borg, *Meeting Jesus Again* and Borg, *Reading the Bible Again*.

heavy burdens, and I will give you rest. Take my yoke upon you, and learn from me; for I am gentle and humble in heart, and you will find rest for your souls. For my yoke is easy, and my burden is light." In another place, he criticizes the scribes and Pharisees because "they tie up heavy burdens, hard to bear, and lay them on the shoulders of others; but they themselves are unwilling to lift a finger to move them" (Matt 23:4). Jesus is not like them. Far from being too heavy, the call to discipleship, as evidenced in the Lord's Prayer and elsewhere, is a light burden.

Make no mistake: discipleship is serious business, and one should not enter into it lightly. It requires commitment and perseverance. "No one who puts a hand to the plow and looks back," Jesus warns, "is fit for the kingdom of God" (Luke 9:62). But once one does make that commitment, one discovers that participation in the kingdom provides gratification and fulfillment like nothing else. Because Jesus's program seeks to build community, one also finds that many hands do indeed make light work.

That work, as we have seen throughout this book, is to join God in the world, where God works tirelessly to bring justice, renewal, and reconciliation. The Lord's Prayer is a staunchly this-worldly manifesto. We address our Prayer to "our Father who art in heaven," but we could just as truly say, "Our Father who *aren't* in heaven," because God has vacated the heaven ghetto in favor of the world God loves. Jesus has eschewed the heavenly hammock and continues his work down here, through his church and in the power of the Spirit, to advance the reign of God.

God is holy, and we honor God's holiness not only by not misusing God's name in idle talk, but also by doing things that reflect God's character and will. In the Prayer we ask for God's kingdom to come and God's will to be done on earth as it is in heaven. By our "amen" we indicate our readiness to implement God's will and take action on behalf of God's kingdom, regardless of the consequences to ourselves.

We also offer petitions about very practical matters: bread, debts, and temptation. Asking God to provide tomorrow's bread today simultaneously expresses trust in God as our provider and laments that we live in a world where too many people don't know where their next meal will come from. Our "amen" to this petition signifies our willingness to engage in service to the hungry and to advocate on their behalf. We tell God and God's hungry children that we stand in solidarity with them and that we will act to subvert and break down the structures that prevent all the world from sharing in God's plenty.

When we say "amen" to the petition about debts, we again commit ourselves to subversive action. God has opened our eyes to the many ways the Domination System uses indebtedness to enrich itself and keep the poor in perpetual bondage. With our "amen" we declare that we want to be part of Jesus's renewed community where the predatory practices of the world do not hold sway. We wish to join this community that recognizes God's sovereignty and ownership, practices jubilee within its own ranks, and models jubilee in the wider world.

Our "amen" to the third petition shows that we see through the lies of the Domination System and refuse to play by its rules anymore. It commits us to creative noncooperation with evil, the exercise of power-with instead of power-over, and the refusal to resort to violence, especially violence in God's name. We renounce the temptation to blaspheme God by using the tools and weapons of the Domination System to advance God's purposes. We know that to do so is to capitulate to the System before we even get started. When we embrace its values and methods, for all intents and purposes we bow down and worship the devil. To this, we shout an unequivocal "No!"

Finally, we say "amen" to the doxology, the part of the Prayer that provides the basis for everything that has come before. We commit ourselves to Jesus's radical agenda, his program of doing justice and building a community characterized by equality, openness, grace, and love, *because* the kingdom and power and glory belong to God and God alone. We owe our ultimate allegiance to God; God's kingdom and will trump any and all lesser allegiances. Jesus and no one else is Lord. Not Caesar, not America, not Wall Street or Madison Avenue, not Hollywood, not the Domination System, and not ourselves. We say "amen" to all of this in hope and joy, trusting that even though we see so much injustice, conflict, hatred, inequality, and heartbreak in the world, all of this too shall be made right.

Do I hear an amen?

LET YOUR YES BE YES AND YOUR NO BE NO

It won't be made right on its own, however. Only God's action can overcome sin, injustice, and evil, and accomplish God's perfect will on earth as in heaven. But in God's overflowing grace, we have a part to play, and "amen" is how we indicate our willingness to accept that role. It's our RSVP to the invitation.

But what then? How do we understand and fulfill these marching orders we have received? The first suggestion I would make, if you find yourself asking that question, is to become an active participant in a community of like-minded persons. Join a local church that takes seriously its calling to "do justice, love kindness, and walk humbly with . . . God" (Mic 6:8). Take part in a small group that combines Bible study and action. If you're in college, get involved with a campus ministry group. Find the arrangement that works best for you; just remember that a healthy Christian disciple does not act alone, but rather in conjunction with others.

Second, find that place where, as Buechner says, your deep hunger and the world's deep need come together. God does not offer a one-size-fits-all, take-it-or-leave-it mandate. God knows what fires your passions, and very likely has something in store for you that will be right up your alley. Seek that in prayer. Identify what you are passionate about. Maybe it's ending hunger or poverty. Become a regular volunteer at a local soup kitchen or food pantry, or join a citizen advocacy group such as Bread for the World. Maybe you want to help disadvantaged children. Scores of non-profit organizations work to improve the lives of kids in need; you could volunteer as a mentor or a tutor. Perhaps interfaith understanding or racial reconciliation is where you want to focus your energy; consider developing friendships with persons outside your ethnic group, or lead your church to participate in interfaith dialogue. You may want to join God's work by helping women with crisis pregnancies; by abolishing the death penalty in your state; by caring for the natural environment; by ministering to people living with HIV or AIDS; by preventing gun violence; or by promoting the arts. And so on. The list really has no limits except those set by our imaginations. As long as the activity promotes the advance of God's reign and provides no aid or comfort to the Domination System, go for it!

Third, persevere in prayer. When we pray, we acknowledge our own limitations and seek access to God's limitless resources. We confess our sins and the ways we have been complicit in the world's evil, both by what we have done and what we have left undone, and seek restoration. We name persons and situations that are beyond our help, and commend them to God, "our refuge and strength, [and] a very present help in trouble" (Ps 46:1). And we recommit ourselves to Jesus's program as outlined in the Lord's Prayer, and seek a renewed vision of the world as it should be, to sustain our hope as we toil our way through the world that is.

In the Sermon of the Mount, Jesus warns his listeners against making oaths. "Do not swear," he says, "either by heaven, for it is the throne of God, or by the earth, for it is his footstool, or by Jerusalem, for it is the city of the great King. . . . Let your word be 'Yes, Yes' or 'No, No'; anything more than this comes from the evil one" (Matt 5:34–37). We find a parallel to this passage in James's epistle: "Above all, my brothers, do not swear, either by heaven or by earth or by any other oath, but let your 'yes' be yes and your 'no' be no, so that you may not fall under condemnation" (Jas 5:12 ESV).

Dietrich Bonhoeffer interprets these admonitions as a call to simplicity of language and straightforwardness of purpose.[2] We are to say what we mean and mean what we say. Honesty must be our *only* policy. If our "yes" means yes and our "no" means no, and if we remain consistent in this over time, we will have no need to embellish our simple word. People will know we are honest and we mean what we say, not because we swear an oath to that effect, but simply because we are honest and mean what we say.

We ought to keep this in mind when we come to the "amen" at the end of the Lord's Prayer. In honesty and simplicity we commit ourselves to Jesus's program—to his countercultural community and to the advance of justice, grace, and the kingdom of God in the world. In honesty and simplicity we say that we understand and accept the challenge of discipleship, and that we want to be a part of what God is doing in the world. The Prayer lays out our marching orders, and in honesty and simplicity we say, "Yes, Lord."

Yes.

2. Bonhoeffer, *Cost of Discipleship*, 135–39.

Bibliography

Apostle's Creed. http://www.creeds.net/ancient/apostles.htm.

Ayo, Nicholas. *The Lord's Prayer: A Survey Theological and Literary.* Notre Dame, IN: University of Notre Dame Press, 1992.

Beiser, Vince. "Seven Big Ways Life Is Getting Better for the World's Poorest." No pages. Online: http://www.takepart.com/article/2014/06/30/what-wonderful-world.

Bezilla, Greg. Personal correspondence with author. June 2, 2014.

Blake, John. "Was Jesus Rich? Swanky Messiah Not Far-Fetched in Prosperity Gospel." *Atlanta Journal-Constitution.* October 22, 2006. Online: http://www.ajc.com/living/content/living/faithandvalues/stories/2006/10/18/1022SLJESUS.html.

Bonhoeffer, Dietrich. *The Cost of Discipleship.* 1937. Reprint, New York: Touchstone, 1995.

Borg, Marcus J. *Meeting Jesus Again for the First Time: The Historical Jesus & the Heart of Contemporary Faith.* San Francisco: HarperSanFrancisco, 1994.

———. *Reading the Bible Again for the First Time: Taking the Bible Seriously but Not Literally.* San Francisco: HarperSanFrancisco, 2001.

Borg, Marcus J., and John Dominic Crossan. *The Last Week.* San Francisco: HarperSanFrancisco, 2006.

Bread for the World. "About Hunger." No pages. Online: http://www.bread.org/hunger.

Browning, Robert. "Pippa's Song." In *English Poetry III: From Tennyson to Whitman.* The Harvard Classics. New York: P.F. Collier & Son, 1909–14; Bartleby.com, 2001. No pages. Online: www.bartleby.com/42/666.html.

Bruderhof. "The Bruderhof." No pages. Online: http://www.bruderhof.com/en.

Brueggeman, Walter. *Genesis.* Interpretation: A Bible Commentary for Teaching and Preaching. Atlanta: John Knox, 1982.

Bruner, Frederick Dale. *The Christbook, Matthew 1–12.* Revised & Expanded Edition. Grand Rapids: Eerdmans, 2004.

Buechner, Frederick. *Godric.* New York: Atheneum, 1980.

———. *Wishful Thinking: A Seeker's ABC.* San Francisco: HarperSanFrancisco, 1973.

Burgess, John P. *The East German Church and the End of Communism.* New York: Oxford University Press, 1997.

Buzby, Jean C., Hodan Farah Wells, and Jeffrey Hyman. "The Estimated Amount, Value, and Calories of Postharvest Food Losses at the Retail and Consumer Levels in the United States." United States Department of Agriculture Economic Research Service. Economic Information Bulletin No. (EIB-121), February 2014. Online: http://www.ers.usda.gov/media/1282296/eib121.pdf.

Byassee, Jason. "The New Monastics: Alternative Christian Communities." *The Christian Century*, 122:21 (2005), 38–47.

Cockburn, Bruce. "If I Had a Rocket Launcher." *Stealing Fire*. True North, 1984. Compact disc.

Crossan, John Dominic. *The Birth of Christianity: Discovering What Happened in the Years Immediately after the Execution of Jesus*. San Francisco: HarperSanFrancisco, 1998.

———. *The Greatest Prayer*. New York: HarperOne, 2010.

———. *The Historical Jesus: The Life of a Mediterranean Jewish Peasant*. San Francisco: HarperSanFrancisco, 1991.

———. *Who Killed Jesus? Exposing the Roots of Anti-Semitism in the Gospel Story of the Death of Jesus*. San Francisco: HarperSanFrancisco, 1995.

Daniel Amos. "It's Sick." *Vox Humana*. Comp. Terry Taylor. Refuge, 1984. Compact disc.

Dennis, Marie, Renny Golden, and Scott Wright, editors. *Oscar Romero: Reflections on His Life and Writings*. Maryknoll, NY: Orbis Books, 2000.

Dwight, John Sullivan. "O Holy Night." Public domain, 1855.

The Episcopal Church. "Holy Eucharist, Rite II." *The Book of Common Prayer and Administration of the Sacraments and Other Rites and Ceremonies of the Church*. New York: Church Hymnal Corporation, 1979.

Goodstein, Laurie. "Robertson Suggests U.S. Kill Venezuela's Leader." *The New York Times*. August 24, 2005. Online: http://www.nytimes.com/2005/08/24/politics/24robertson.html?_r=0.

Horsley, Richard A. *Bandits, Prophets, and Messiahs: Popular Movements at the Time of Jesus*. With John S. Hanson. Minneapolis: Winston, 1985.

———. *Jesus in Context: Power, People, & Performance*. Minneapolis: Fortress, 2008.

The Innocence Mission. "Every Hour Here." *Umbrella*. Comp. Karen Peris. A&M, 1991. Compact disc.

Jeremias, Joachim. *Rediscovering the Parables*. New York: Scribner's, 1966.

Joel, Billy. "Only the Good Die Young." *The Stranger*. Family Productions/Columbia, 1977. LP.

Josephus, Flavius. *The Wars of the Jews, or History of the Destruction of Jerusalem* [*War*]. Translated by William Whiston. Public Domain. Kindle edition.

King Jr., Martin Luther. "I See the Promised Land." In *A Testament of Hope: The Essential Writings of Martin Luther King, Jr.*, edited by James M. Washington, 279–86. San Francisco: HarperSanFrancisco, 1986.

———. *Strength to Love*. Philadelphia: Fortress Press, 1963.

Lasswell, Harold D. *Politics: Who Gets What, When, How*. New York: McGraw-Hill, 1936.

The Letter of the Smyrnaeans or the Martyrdom of Polycarp. Translated by J.B. Lightfoot. 1990. Adapted and modified. No pages. Online: http://www.earlychristianwritings.com/text/martyrdompolycarp–lightfoot.html.

Levine, Amy-Jill. *The Misunderstood Jew: The Church and the Scandal of the Jewish Jesus*. San Francisco: HarperSanFrancisco, 2006.

Lewis, C. S. *The Lion, the Witch, and the Wardrobe*. New York: HarperEntertainment, 1950.

Martyn, J. Louis. *History and Theology in the Fourth Gospel*. 3rd ed. Louisville: Westminster John Knox, 2003.

McLaren, Brian D. *Everything Must Change: Jesus, Global Crises, and a Revolution of Hope*. Nashville: Thomas Nelson, 2007.

Mullins, Rich. "Quoting Deuteronomy to the Devil." *Brother's Keeper*. Comps. Rich Mullins and Beaker. Reunion, 1995. Compact disc.

Myers, Ched. *The Biblical Vision of Sabbath Economics*. Washington: The Church of the Savior, 2001.

Newman Jr., Barclay M. *A Concise Greek-English Dictionary of the New Testament*. Stuttgart: Biblia-Druck, 1971.

Niebuhr, Reinhold. *The Nature and Destiny of Man: A Christian Interpretation. Volume I: Human Nature*. New York: Scribner's, 1942.

Pfeifer, Kimberly, Gawain Kripke, and Emily Alpert. *Finding the Moral Fiber: Why Reform Is Urgently Needed for a Fair Cotton Trade*. Oxfam Briefing Paper 69 (October 2004).

Plato. *Phaedo*. Translated by Benjamin Jowett. 2008. The Gutenberg Project. No pages. Online: http://www.gutenberg.org/files/1658/1658-h/1658-h.htm.

R.E.M. *Murmur*. I.R.S., 1983. Compact disc.

Romero. DVD. Directed by John Duigan. Produced by Paulist Pictures, 1989. Lansdale, PA: Vision Video, 2009.

Rossing, Barbara R. *The Rapture Exposed: The Message of Hope in the Book of Revelation*. New York: Basic Books, 2004.

Shelley, John C. "Money." In *Mercer Dictionary of the Bible*. Edited by Watson E. Mills, 581. Macon, GA: Mercer University Press, 1990.

Springsteen, Bruce. "Atlantic City." *Nebraska*. Columbia, 1982. Compact disc.

Stassen, Glen H. "Christian Ethics." Lecture presented at The Southern Baptist Theological Seminary, Louisville, KY, September 20, 1994.

———. *Just Peacemaking: Transforming Initiatives for Justice and Peace*. Louisville: Westminster/John Knox, 1992.

Stassen, Glen H., and David P. Gushee. *Kingdom Ethics: Following Jesus in Contemporary Context*. Downers Grove, IL: InterVarsity, 2003.

Three Days of the Condor. DVD. Directed by Sydney Pollack. Produced by Dino De Laurentiis Company, 1975. Hollywood, CA: Paramount Home Video, 1999.

Tolkien, J.R.R. *The Lord of the Rings*. Boston: Houghton Mifflin, 1955.

Twain, Mark. "The Man That Corrupted Hadleyburg." In *The Man That Corrupted Hadleyburg and Other Stories and Essays*, 11–83. New York: Harper & Brothers, 1905. Online: https://ia600504.us.archive.org/16/items/mancomputedootwairich/mancomputedootwairich_bw.pdf.

The Usual Suspects. VHS. Directed by Bryan Singer. Produced by PolyGram Filmed Entertainment, 1995. Beverly Hills, CA: MGM Home Entertainment, 1999.

Webb, Derek. "A Love That's Stronger Than Our Fear." *The Ringing Bell*. INO, 2007. Compact disc.

———. "This Too Shall Be Made Right." *The Ringing Bell*. INO, 2007. Compact disc.

Weil, Simone. *The Notebooks of Simone Weil*. Translated by Arthur Wills. London: Routledge and Kegan Paul, 1956. Reprinted. New York: Routledge, 2004. Page references are to the 2004 edition.

Wink, Walter. *Engaging the Powers*. Minneapolis: Fortress, 1992.

World Council of Churches. *Confessing the One Faith: An Ecumenical Explication of the Apostolic Faith As It Is Confessed in the Nicene–Constantinopolitan Creed (381)*. Faith and Order Paper No. 153. Geneva: WCC Publications, n.d.

World Food Programme. "Hunger." No pages. Online: http://www.wfp.org/hunger/faqs.

World Health Organization. "Global Health Observatory: Under-Five Mortality." No pages. Online: http://www.who.int/gho/child_health/mortality/mortality_under_five/en/.